# I AM DESTINED FOR ISAAC

## WALKING IN GOD'S PROMISES

# LILLIANIS J CRUZ

# I AM DESTINED FOR ISAAC



**Published by**:
Gracehouse Publishing
56, Gosport Road, Walthamstow,
London, United Kingdom, E17 7LY

Unless otherwise indicated, all Scripture quotations are taken from the New King James Version (NKJV) of the Bible.

# DEDICATION

I dedicate this book to my late Pastor, Tony Mendez. March 30th, 2017, the last day I saw him alive, was the day that God gave me the word about writing a book. Although Pastor Tony cannot physically read this book, was able to see me preach, or met Isaak in person, he planted the seeds that are germinating through this book and my family's ministry. He saw the preacher, he saw the entrepreneur, he saw the writer and he saw the mother; he saw all that I would be and saw God's promise fulfilled in my life before I saw it with my own eyes. He believed in me but most of all, he believed in the promises God had for my life.

I AM DESTINED FOR ISAAC

# CONTENTS

# INTRODUCTION

I started to write this book following a word confirmed to me by God on September 24, 2017. I was pregnant with Isaak, my son, at the moment. I was carrying my promise within. The word was given to me at the very end of our second Sunday service, unexpected, through a fifteen year old young man at my church. I was already in the midst of writing another book but God spoke to my heart and told me that the book He was talking about during that prophecy was not the book I was writing at the time. The book I was previously writing ended up in my current blog, Hearing from the Throne, which has been active since January 2018, for the glory of God.

*I am destined for Isaac* was birthed from a preaching, and such preaching was born from a simple quote the Lord placed in my heart. God placed the quote "Doing things your way can give birth to an Ishmael when God destined you to birth an Isaac." God had to speak to me in such a way as I was trying to have a child for 7 months and nothing would happen. I can only imagine the pain many men and women experience as they have to wait even longer to conceive. I was doing everything "I was supposed to do" and I had the "perfect" timeline for when I was supposed to have this baby. I had planned the year 2017 so "perfectly" but God had other plans. I am not saying that it is wrong to plan or have goals. I am a very goal-oriented and determined person. During that season, I mistakenly used these gifts God had deposited within me to dictate God's will for my life.  I thought that I could accomplish all of my plans through my own ability and in my own timing. I honestly did not add God to the equation of my plans. Coming to this realization led me to repentance and transformed my life. I pray that such realizations change your life as well.

It was not until June 2017 that I realized that I couldn't do things my way anymore and I just had to let God do what He wanted to do in my life. It was in June 2017 when I truly held on to the promise that God had given me of having a child and I made a decision in my heart to patiently wait for God to fulfill this promise. It was the month in which I made that decision that I actually became pregnant. The promise was beginning to be unfolded. Just when my faith was starting to dwindle, I decided to wait and my faith started to increase.

If I am honest with you, I did not think I could write an entire book out of a simple outline from a preaching.

However, I came to the realization that this book comes from the heart of God himself; He's the author, I am just the instrument He used to place it on paper. I am grateful to the many people who also deposited words of encouragement and wisdom through my process of waiting on God's promise. As I write, you will notice that I quote a few of them.

This book will take you through the life of Abraham, Sarah and many other people in the Bible, people like you and I, who were given a promise by God and whose lives were transformed as they waited on the fulfilment of God's promises. I pray that this book is a blessing to your life and helps you learn to walk in God's promises. Waiting is not easy, trust me, I am not the most patient person myself. However, I learned through my process that God continues to remain faithful to His promises, no matter how long I have to wait. He developed patience in my life and allowed me to know him as the God who fulfills His promises. He prepared my heart to receive, embrace and nurture my promise. God taught me how to wait in Him, and trust me, it was worth the wait.

# Chapter 1

# A PROMISE IS GIVEN

*"But Sarai was barren; she had no child."* Genesis 11:30

*"Now the Lord had said to Abram: "Get out of your country, from your family and from your father's house, to the land that I will show you. I will make you a great nation; I will bless you and make your name great; and you shall be a blessing. I will bless those who bless you, and I will curse him who curses you; and in you all the families of the earth shall be blessed." So Abram departed as the Lord had spoken to him, and Lot went with him. And Abram was seventy-five years old when he departed from Haran. Then Abram took Sarai his wife and Lot his brother's son, and all their possessions that they had gathered, and the people whom they had acquired in Haran, and they departed to go to the land of Canaan. So they came to the land of Canaan. Abram passed through the land to the place of Shechem, as far as the terebinth tree of Moreh. And the Canaanites were then in the land. Then the*

*Lord appeared to Abram and said, "To your descendants I will give this land".* Genesis 12: 1-7

We become aware of Abraham in Genesis 11 as the Bible describes the descendants of Terah. One verse that caught my attention was Genesis 11:30 *"But Sarai was barren; she had no child."* This verse is key to understanding why God's promise might seem bizarre to anyone hearing about it. This verse is also key to understanding the beauty and magnitude of the promise made to Abraham.

## WHAT IS A PROMISE?

Before I continue writing, I wanted to understand what a promise is. We hear this word a lot, especially in church, but do we truly have an understanding of what a promise is? A promise is defined as *"a declaration or assurance that one will do a particular thing or that a particular thing will happen"*.[1] A promise is a commitment that an action will be taken or that something will be given. There is really not much of a difference between what a promise means in the secular world and what it means in the Bible, it is simply the assurance that something will happen.

Now, the difference between a man-made promise and a God-made promise is that God's promises will come to pass as He is faithful in His nature. The Bible says in

______

[1] https://en.oxforddictionaries.com/definition/promise

Hebrew 10:23 that "He who promised is Faithful". We can have the assurance that God will fulfill His promises because He will not go against His own nature. Understanding this gives us the ability to trust God at all times, even when things seem to be working contrary to our expected promises. We do not have to live life in a constant state of anxiety when we learn to understand the faithfulness of God. Even if a man has the intention of fulfilling a promise, due to our fallen nature, man has the high possibility of not fulfilling a promise. As humans, we all have been guilty of falling short when it comes to fulfilling a promise.

I do believe that there are promises that are conditional, meaning that an action is required from your part in order for God to fulfill that promise in your life. This is not to say that God is not all powerful and that He cannot fulfill a promise without requiring something from us. There are some promises that are unconditional, meaning that they shall come to pass regardless of what we do or stop doing. However, I would like to focus on conditional promises for a minute. Notice how God begins the promise to Abraham by telling him "Get out of your country and go to the land I will show you" and then He continues by telling Abraham that He will make of him a great nation. While I do believe that God could have made Abraham a great nation right where he was, Abraham needed to engage in an act of *obedience* and run with this promise.

God's promises do not just stay as promises but they lead to covenants. The promise made to Abraham did not just stay as a promise rather it later became a covenant between him and God. In Genesis 17:2, God makes a covenant with Abraham after He had promised him multiple times that He would make a great nation of him. A covenant is a relationship; it requires for both parties to be involved. God asks for Abraham to walk blamelessly before Him and He establishes a covenant, or relationship, with him. At this point, God was not just a God who made promises rather He became a relational God to Abraham. God is telling Abraham, "I do not just want to make you a promise, I want to have a relationship with you". God is not only a God of *Promises*, he is a God of *Covenants*. He wants to have an intimate relationship with you! God considered Abraham His friend, as it is stated in James 2:23, indicating a relationship.

When it comes to God's promises, we need to understand that God will not always show us *how* He will fulfill His promise in our lives right away. He can guarantee that He will but it is the journey that unfolds how God will fulfill the promise. If God told you every detail right away, then there will not be a need for faith. In Hebrews 11:1 we learn that "faith is the substance of things hoped for, the evidence of things *not seen*". If you already saw the method by which God was going to fulfill His promise, then faith wouldn't be a requirement. We believe God's promises by *faith*. We believe that God Himself exists by *faith*. When walking towards your promises, you will face situations that look very contrary to the promise expected. Abraham pointed this out to God on Genesis 15 and stated the obvious: "Lord, you have given me no offspring". Your path towards your promise will not always make sense to you but God will make a way. His ways are not our ways, His thoughts are much higher than what we can even begin to imagine. I believe in a God who makes a way when there is no way. I believe in a God who can spring water in the driest desert, light fire on an altar full of water and make a ninety year old give birth!

One last point to remember about promises is that God's promises are not only to bless you but also to make you a blessing. In Genesis 12:2 the Lord tells Abraham *"I will bless you and make your name great; and you shall be a blessing."* Not only the fulfillment of the promise is what allows us to become a blessing but what we learn through our process of waiting can make us a blessing as well. I was encouraged many times by others who waited to see God's promises, even though they had not seen their own promise yet. Your promise will bless you, your household and those you encounter as well. My late pastor, Tony Mendez, used to say "I am blessed to bless". I never want to be so selfish that all I care about is being blessed without wanting to be a blessing to others. Remember, we await for our promises not only because they will be a blessing to us but because others shall partake of the blessings that are tied to those promises.

In conclusion, a promise is the assurance that something will come to pass. God is faithful to fulfill His promise because faithfulness is part of His nature. Because promises lead to covenants, God wants to have a relationship with us and such relationship will require acts of obedience from our part. Last but not least, your promise is intended to bless you and those around you.

## GOD GAVE ME A PROMISE, THEN WHAT?

Now that we understand what a promise is and what it can lead to, what do we do? There are multiple things you can do with the promise that God has given you. Despite the many options, it is important to rely on the Holy Spirit to know what to do after a promise is given to us. When a promise is given, you can run with it, learn to let go, wait, become paralyzed or even hide. I will not tell you what to do as that is the Holy Spirit's job, but I will explain each of your options in detail.

## RUN WITH IT

As I have stated before, some promises will require action from your part. One of the many options you have when a promise is given is to *run* with it. Abraham ran with his promise. In Genesis 12:4 we read that *"Abram departed as the*

*Lord had spoken to him, and Lot went with him. And Abram was seventy-five years old when he departed from Haran. Then Abram took Sarai his wife and Lot his brother's son, and all their possessions that they had gathered, and the people whom they had acquired in Haran, and they departed to go to the land of Canaan".* Abraham did not waste time after his promise was given! While we cannot tell exactly how long it took him to run with this promise, we can assume that he took almost immediate action to follow God's instructions.

There will be some promises that have instructions tied to them and will require immediate action. God Himself will tell you what to do in order to see the promise fulfilled and He will order your steps as you walk or run towards that promise. When God told me to write this book, He gave me a glimpse of the outcome of it. Despite the glimpse, I had to take action and start writing it. Not even twenty four hours after getting the instructions to write this book, I received the title and the outline of the entire book. I had a task to complete in order to walk towards the promises that God had given me.

I encourage you to think about the promises that God has given you and ask the Holy Spirit for direction in regards to those promises. Perhaps God made you promises but you took another action when God needed you to run with that promise. If you stayed stagnant, it is not too late. Start running with the promise the Lord gave you, if that is the direction that the Spirit is leading you to. Do not worry about who thinks you are crazy. I am sure that Abraham's family thought that he was crazy for picking up everything and leaving at the age of seventy five! However, Abraham did not seem to care about this because he knew that God had made him a promise.

On May 28, 2017, the Lord reminded me that He had promised me a child and He gave me a clear instruction in regards to it. God said "start buying clothes (baby clothes)". On May 29, 2017 I went to the local department store and bought a onesie for a baby boy, as I knew in my heart that my first born would be a boy. Two weeks later I bought a cute set of boy pajamas and I showed them to someone very close to me. Their initial reaction was to say "stop buying baby clothes because you do not know if it [getting pregnant] will happen soon and I don't want you to get your hopes up". In my humanity, my heart was shattered in a million pieces. I even cried. But later my spirit rejoiced because I knew that this meant that my promise was even closer! My encouragement to you, do not worry about what others will think as long as you know that God has given you an instruction. Just run with it.

## LET GO

A second option, or even requirement, when you are given a promise is to *let go*. Abraham not only ran with the promise but he had to let go of his family and his land. I can imagine that this must have been difficult for him.

However, there was one small problem and the Bible makes very clear mention of it: Abraham took Lot with him. From a cultural standpoint, Lot was Abraham's next of kin; he was Abraham's nearest blood relative. Lot's father, Abraham's brother had died and he was under the care of Abraham and his father Terah. I wonder if Abraham thought that God would give him descendants via Lot, being that he was his next of kin.

In Genesis 13 we can read that Lot had great possessions as well as Abraham, which meant that they could not dwell in the land together anymore. This relationship started to bring strife between them. Later on we learn that Abraham had to go into battle in Sodom and Gomorrah to be able to save Lot. Taking Lot with him led him to fight a battle that was not his.

When God says it is time to let go of everything, He means everything and everyone. Many times we want for God to fulfill His promise but we want to take many "Lots" along the way. It made sense for Abraham to take Lot along, but it was not what was asked of him. Taking Lot did not disable the promise from being fulfilled but it sure brought Abraham unnecessary trouble. While our fulfilled promises could be a blessing to others, not everyone is meant to go with us as we walk into our promises. It can be painful but it is a reality. I am sure that God has many other amazing promises for the people we had to leave behind; they are not exempt from the promises of God just because you had to leave them behind due to your obedience to God.

We need discernment to know who will go with us or who we need to let go of. It does not mean that we do not love these individuals, it just means that it was not God's plan for them to go to the places that God had intended for us to go. Jesus Himself had twelve disciples yet only John was present while He was fulfilling his purpose by dying on the Cross. Do not allow your emotional connections or soul ties to delay you as you walk into your promise.

If God is demanding for you to leave something or someone behind, it is time to do so. At times God may actually ask you to leave attitudes and behaviors behind in order to successfully walk into the promise He has for you. In my case, I needed to let go of disbelief in order to learn to move forward based on the promise that God had given me. Only when I let go of disbelief is when I found contentment in just waiting as my promise arrived.

## WAIT

Another action we can take is to *wait* for our promises. As I typed that last sentence I wondered "How can you take action by waiting?". It is possible. The word "wait" is a verb, which indicates action. There will be times in which all you can do is wait for your promise. You have let go of what you needed to let go of, you are running with the promise but then comes a time in which all you can do is wait on the Lord. We tend to misunderstand waiting for the lack of action. However, as believers, we can continue to praise God as our promise comes, we continue to pray, we continue to meditate on the word of God, we continue to serve, all while we wait on the Lord. I will go more in detail about this in further chapters.

Those who wait upon the Lord shall renew their strength! (Isaiah 40:31) Waiting leads you to a season of preparation that running and letting go cannot get you to. The testing of your faith produces perseverance (James 1:3) and many times the perseverance that you develop as you are waiting will be necessary to withstand certain processes that come with your promise.

## HIDING

As I was meditating upon the option of hiding, I thought it wouldn't have been a good option to hide as you wait for the promise. However, the Holy Spirit started to show me that there have been times in which people in the Bible needed to hide in order to successfully get to their promise. Take David for example. David had to be in hiding for many years, even though he was promised that he was going to be king by the Lord Himself. He understood that he was facing persecution and he had to go through a season of hiding, led by the Lord, as he waited to be king. Many times we will need to learn how to hide under the wings of our Father (Psalm 17:8). This is a place of safety, comfort and intimacy in which we increase in wisdom for when we get to the promise.

## PARALYSIS

The last option that you have is to become *paralyzed*. To become paralyzed is to be incapable of movement. It is not the same as waiting since, as stated before, waiting is not necessarily the lack of action. The people of Israel became paralyzed in front of the Red Sea. Moses himself told them in Exodus 14:13 to stand still but God replies to him by saying "tell the children of Israel to move forward". If the people of Israel would have decided to stay paralyzed, they would have perished by the hand of the Egyptians and not reached their promised land. There will be times in which the Lord will tell you "be still and know that I am God" (Psalms 46:10). Such stillness doesn't come out of fear but out of trust in the Lord. Paralysis comes out of fear, out of too much analysis. And analysis comes out of a place of trying to find logic within events that only God can do. Only God could part the Red Sea. Only God can take you through, and within that taking through, you may have to run, wait, be still, let go or hide for a season.

You may be saying to yourself "but God has not given me a promise". However, God has given each one of us promises that can be found in His Word. There are collective promises, meaning that they apply to all of God's people and there are individual promises. The options discussed above could apply to both collective and individual promises. My hope is that you seek guidance from the Holy Spirit to know if you have to run with a promise, learn to let go, wait for the promise, be still or even hide.

# *Chapter 2*

# DOUBT

*"After these things the word of the Lord came to Abram in a vision, saying, "Do not be afraid, Abram. I am your shield, your exceedingly great reward." But Abram said, "Lord God, what will you give me, seeing I go childless, and the heir of my house is Eliezer of Damascus?" Then Abram said, "Look, you have given me no offspring; indeed one born in my house is my heir!" And behold, the word of the Lord came to him, saying, "This one shall not be your heir, but one who will come from your own body shall be your heir." Genesis 15:1-4*

You have been given a promise and now you are living and walking according to the direction in which the Lord is leading you in your journey to that promise. What happens when doubt starts creeping in? What happens when your faith dwindles? What happens when your natural eyes are not seeing what God has promised?

In our humanity, it can be difficult to understand the supernatural. If you are anything like me, you may want answers right away and may want logical answers to illogical questions. I can definitely identify with Abraham when he tells the Lord "Look, you have given me no offspring; indeed one born in my house is my heir!". To Abraham, it only made sense for Eliezer to be his heir as he was childless. It is not illogical to think this, honestly. It was culturally acceptable for Eliezer to be the heir during those times. Abraham was pointing out the logical to a Supernatural God! Many of us find ourselves "pointing out the obvious" to God. Trust me, God will not get mad at you for doing it; He will see this as an opportunity to remind you of His promise and remind you that He is more than able to fulfill the promise He gave you. I find comfort in God's reply to Abraham when He says "This one shall not be your heir, but one who will come from your own body shall be your heir."

Doubt is an emotion that tends to creep in when our eyes can't see what we are waiting for. I went on a quest to find several definitions of doubt. I found that doubt means being uncertain of something, lack of conviction and even fear. While it can be concluded that doubt is being uncertain about something, it can be manifested in different ways. Doubt can be manifested in *fear*, *desperation* and even *mocking*. I can say without a doubt that Abraham at one point must have felt fear as he saw that he was aging, as he saw that Sarai was aging, and they would go childless. I lived through the fear of thinking that I was not going to have a child, or that I would end up like Sarah, having a child at a "late age".

## FEAR

God giving you  a promise does not make you exempt from doubting it. Doubt in reality is a human emotion. We sometimes have the tendency to feel guilty for doubting. God knew already that doubt was a possibility when He gives us a promise and that is why He constantly reminds us of His promise. There are countless times in which God had to tell Joshua, "be strong and courageous, do not fear". God even reminds us multiple times in the Bible to not fear for He will be with us. If doubt and fear would not be a common emotion, God would not have the need to remind us to not fear so many times. Do not feel guilty for feeling doubtful, that is exactly what the enemy wants. He will try to dump guilt on top of your doubt, which might just make things worse. A good option when in doubt would be to pray for God to provide you peace as you wait, continue to reassure and remind you of His promise. I have a tendency of writing every single promise God has made me in my journal. This way I can easily access what God has said when time starts to pass by and doubt starts to creep in.

Doubt can become a paralyzing agent as we walk into our promises. It can make you freeze when you are supposed to keep moving. Stormie Ormartian wrote in her book *The Power of a Praying Wife* "there is a difference between a fearful thought that comes to mind as a prompting to pray for a particular thing, and a tormenting spirit of fear that paralyzes." As stated before, fear is a human response to a perceived threat. However, we need to learn to pray about these fears rather than allowing them to paralyze us. Pray that God may give you the courage to continue moving forward, in whichever way you have to, towards the promises that He has made you.

In life, we might experience certain hiccups as we journey through our promise. In the natural sense, a hiccup is a contraction that interrupts your normal breathing. In the spiritual sense, a hiccup is any given situation or word spoken that attempts to disrupt your faith. There will be situations, people or even words spoken over your life that will be painful and will make you lose sight of God's promise for a few seconds. These hiccups may come in the form of well intended but painful words; words that force you to rely on your reality versus maintaining your sight in God's reality. Doubt in the spiritual sense is essentially that; focusing on your human reality and losing sight of God's reality. When spoken over our lives, these words feel like we are out of air. They interrupt our faith for just a few moments that actually feel like an eternity. We wonder, "will I ever believe again the same way I did? What if I am crazy and I am just acting upon my emotions rather than my faith? Did I hear God right or are the words coming out of this person's mouth true?"

My pastor used to say "to see wonders, you have to do things that make people wonder". This means proclaiming things as they are even though you cannot see them yet. This means walking in faith to a promised land you cannot see yet. This means celebrating the arrival of your miracle even though you cannot see it yet. Many times people will think we are crazy for this but that is how faith works. I remember God telling me once "I am giving you ideas and things to do because you are crazy enough to do them." This word was encouraging because I understood that sometimes I will make people wonder about what I am doing but I am acting on my faith. God's agenda for our lives sometimes does not fit our personal timeline. However, God's perfect timing will always yield a greater blessing. While doubt is a normal human emotion, do not allow for this life's hiccups to make your faith stumble.

Do not allow for your doubt to turn into unbelief. At one point I thought that these two words meant the same. However, I learned that doubt is questioning your faith while unbelief is not believing at all. You cannot doubt what you do not already believe. In Matthew 14 we see the story of Peter walking on water. At first his faith was at its peak. He got off the boat to walk on water when no one else would. He became afraid and started to *doubt.* However, even in his doubt he *believed* Jesus could save him. Jesus' reply is what catches my attention. In verse 31 Jesus says "you of little faith, why did you doubt?". This answer does not imply that Peter stopped believing rather that Peter's faith was decreased by the fear and doubt that started to take place.

Now, if you allow for such doubt to take root in your heart, it can actually turn into an absolute lack of faith, leading to unbelief. Unbelief can lead us to not receive the words that God is trying to speak upon our lives. Michael Dow says in his book *Fasting: Rediscovering the Ancient Pathways* that:

> *"There will be seasons of your life where God will not be able to talk about certain things because of the unbelief that has taken up residency in your heart. Because of this unbelief, if He were to speak about certain things, they would simply fall to the ground because you would not be willing to believe them."*

Many times we wonder why God is not reminding us of His promises or why He is not giving us a "fresh word" from heaven. But why would God continue to remind someone of promises they are unwilling to believe in? I mean, God in his mercy still does but sometimes we tend to miss the fullness of what He is saying due to our lack of faith.

## DESPERATION

> *"Now Sarai, Abram's wife, had borne him no children. And she had an Egyptian maidservant whose name was Hagar. So Sarai said to Abram, "See now, the Lord has restrained me from bearing children. Please, go into the maid; perhaps I shall obtain children by her." And Abram heeded to the voice of Sarai"* Genesis 16:1-2

Desperation is another manifestation of doubt. Most of us at one point have experienced desperation. Some of us even experience it on a daily basis. Whether is traffic, slow paced people, waiting for a package to arrive, we have experienced desperation in one way or another. The problem with desperation is that it could lead you to find "solutions" that could make the problem worse. Have you ever taken a "shortcut" to your destination thinking it would get you there faster and ended up taking longer to get there? That is a perfect example of what I am talking about.

Sarai started to become desperate because she would not conceive. It had been approximately 11 years since God had promised Abraham that he would have a child. Honestly, who could blame her? She probably thought that her "biological clock" was ticking fast and she was going to miss her chance on motherhood. So many years had passed since God made her a promise and she probably resigned to watch that promise be fulfilled through someone else.

Don't forget, the promise that God has given you shall be fulfilled through your generation, through your very own family.

Sarai's plan seemed simple and logical; she would have her maid have a child and she would raise him as her own. Not only was Sarai's plan logical, it was actually part of the marital customs of her time. According to Samuel J. Schultz's writings on his book *The Old Testament Speaks*, it was not uncommon for marriages to have these arrangements with their servants. There was nothing essentially wrong with doing this. I see many mothers who have not been able to conceive and engage in the beautiful journey of adoption, surrogacy, fostering, etc. However, this is not what Sarai was told to do. She did something that seemed "good", that was customary of her time, but only as a result of desperation. You see, those things that seem good, if they are done out of desperation, can actually turn into a curse. The outcome of Sarai's desperate move affects even our current generation. Do not allow for your desperation to lead you to bad decision making. Pray that God may grant you patience and clothe yourself with patience on a daily basis as you journey towards the fulfillment of your promise.

By no means I am trying to bring shame to Sarai. In the end, she was human and I am sure we have all made these mistakes at one point. My goal is for us to learn from Sarai's own experience. Sarai forgot about one key feature of her marriage. Genesis 2:24 says "Therefore a man shall leave his father and mother and be joined to his wife, and they shall become *one flesh*." Abraham and Sarah were one. Therefore; when God tells Abraham in Genesis 15:6 *"but one who will come from your own body shall be your heir"*, that statement applied to Sarai as well. The promise that God has given you applies to your marriage, your household and your future generation. For those who are in ministry, maybe you think that the promise of ministry was made to just your spouse, but that promise applies to both of you. You are not insignificant in that promise being fulfilled rather you are an essential part of its fulfillment. You may not be the one actively in ministry at the moment but your support towards your spouse allows for that promise to be fulfilled as well. Without Sarah, there was Ishmael, with Sarah, there was Isaac.

All in all, do not allow for desperation to take root in your heart and lead you to create fleshly solutions to fulfill a heavenly promise. If you are struggling with desperation, always remember that Isaiah 40:31 states that *"those who wait upon the Lord shall renew their strength, shall mount up with wings like eagles, shall run and not be weary, they shall walk and not faint"*. (NKJV). As you wait, you shall regain strength to continue walking towards the promise. You will not faint. Do not heed to desperation.

*"...and Abram heeded to the voice of Sarai."* Genesis 16:2

Sarai portrayed her attitude of desperation to her husband. At times our own desperation will show even through our pores. Desperation is a result of doubt and yes, we are bound to get desperate at times. Are we infecting those around us with that same desperation? As I waited for my baby to come, I remember crying to my husband and expressing how I felt. Not infecting others with your own desperation does not mean that you will not be able to express your feelings to others. During this process, I had to discern between expressing my feelings to my husband, praying about them or writing about them. I could not share everything that I was feeling to my husband because I did not want to infect him with my doubt nor plant a seed of desperation upon his heart. Desperation will come from time to time, just do not infect others with your own. I am grateful that God guarded my husband's heart against desperation. I have to admit, he is way more patient than I am and I believe that helped him stay grounded too. He was very supportive as I cried and always reminded me of God's promises upon our lives.

Now, you might have people in your life who may try to infect you with seeds of desperation. When this happens, it is up to you to heed to what I like to call "the voice of Sarai". The voice of Sarai will tell you at times that your ways are better and you can come up with a better solution than God's solution. This voice will remind you that years have passed and God has not fulfilled His promise so it will be up to you to fulfill that promise. I have witnessed people to whom God has promised a spouse, time passess by and they just marry the first person that comes across their path. I have witnessed others who just make bad business or career decisions out of heeding to the voice of desperation. We need to shut the voices of "Sarai" that are leading to mental battles, that lead to anxiety, that lead to desperation, worry and doubt. Such voices make us forget about the word that God has already deposited over our lives, just like it happened to Abraham. The voice of Sarai will implant a "good solution" in your heart and you heed to it by taking action upon such "good solution".

Another voice that we cannot heed to is the voice of Peninnah. To give you some background, Peninnah was the second wife of Elkanah. His first wife, Hannah, was not able to have children for years and Peninnah would tease her in order to make her angry (1 Samuel 1:6-7). Peninnah's teasing voice would drive Hannah to the point of crying and not eating. Humanly speaking, who wouldn't be affected by someone constantly mocking them? Who wouldn't doubt? There is something we must do to shut the voice of Peninnah. We cannot continue listening to those voices that make fun of us for believing that God can make the impossible possible. Later in the story we see that Hannah arose and prayed to God. She made a vow to God and poured out her soul before Him. God granted her petition as she poured out her heart despite the pain of not having a child. Do not allow the mocking of others to keep you from continuing to pray for your promise, to keep you from pouring out your heart to the Lord. After all, Penninah was most likely making fun of Hannah due to her own insecurities since Penninah was the second wife.

## MOCKING

One last way in which doubt can be manifested is in the form of mocking. Not only did Sarah laughed but Abraham was the first to laugh! Sarah and Abraham mocked or laughed because what the Lord was saying He was going to do seemed impossible. Actually, it didn't seem impossible, it was scientifically impossible. Think about it, in modern day, is it possible for a 100 year old man and a 90 year old woman to conceive naturally? As far as I am aware, there is no cure or pill that can make a 90 year old woman fertile again, let alone a 100 year old man.

There will be times in which God will tell you things that will make you laugh because of some disbelief that has taken root in your heart. On May 6, 2017, God used one of the prophets who attended my church's women's retreat and brought a message to my best friend. She stated that she felt from the Spirit that many young couples were going to conceive in a short time. My best friend was not planning to have a child at that moment; at all. However, she was not the one who mocked. I was. She tells me, of course with the hope that I would be hopeful, since I was the one who had been trying to conceive for the past 6 months. I snorted when she told me that. I would not say it was necessarily because I didn't believe God could do it; contrary to Sarah's situation, it was scientifically possible for me to conceive. I had not received a diagnosis of infertility at that point. I laughed because I said to myself, "If God hasn't done it for the past 6 months, why would He do it now?". I resigned myself to just wait it out and I most definitely did not want to get my hopes up.

Not even a month passed by, and by the end of the month of May 2017, my best friend and another dear friend to me find out that they are pregnant! So many emotions went through my head but one that I clearly remember was a sense of guilt; I felt guilt for laughing at what that prophet said. God did not punish me for laughing though. He had to show me His power in full display and in a different way than He had shown it to my friends. God had to show me that His timing is perfect. By the following month, I was pregnant myself! This came to be a blessing because I was able to share such a beautiful transition with my best friend; the transition from wives to mothers. You best believe that from now on, I do not laugh at anything the Lord tells me, no matter how crazy it sounds, because I know that He is more than capable of making the impossible possible. If you have found yourself in a mocking position, it is not too late. It does not necessarily mean that God will not fulfill His promise.

## WHERE ARE YOU TAKING ME?

*[15] Now on the day that the tabernacle was raised up, the cloud covered the tabernacle, the tent of the Testimony; from evening until morning it was above the tabernacle like the appearance of fire. [16] So it was always: the cloud covered it by day, and the appearance of fire by night. [17] Whenever the cloud was taken up from above the tabernacle, after that the children of Israel would journey; and in the place where the cloud settled, there the children of Israel would pitch their tents. [18] At the command of the Lord the children of Israel would journey, and at the command of the Lord they would camp; as long as the cloud stayed above the tabernacle they remained encamped. [19] Even when the cloud continued long, many days above the tabernacle, the children of Israel kept the charge of the Lord and did not journey. [20] So it was, when the cloud was above the tabernacle a few days: according to the command of the Lord they would remain encamped, and according to the command of the Lord they would journey. [21] So it was, when the cloud remained only from evening until morning: when the cloud was taken up in the morning, then they would journey; whether by day or by night, whenever the cloud was taken up, they would journey. [22] Whether it was two days, a month, or a year that the cloud remained above the tabernacle, the children of Israel would remain encamped and not journey; but when it was taken up, they would journey. [23] At the command of the Lord they remained encamped, and at the command of the Lord they journeyed; they kept the charge of*

*the Lord, at the command of the Lord by the hand of Moses.*
Numbers 9:15-23

There will be times in our journey that we will ask God "where are you taking me?". In this brief passage, the Israelites were guided through the desert on to their promised land. I am sure many of them did not understand why they would set camp for a few days and then leave. Despite all of the moving around, God knew what He was doing and why He was doing it. We tend to get impatient about our journey to the promised land. We have to be reminded on a daily basis that we need God to guide our steps for He knows the way to the promised land. The Israelites would not have been able to make it on their own through the desert. They did not have a map to get to Canaan. They had to learn how to solely and completely rely on God's direction in order to make it to the land that was promised to them.

There are deserts that the Lord has to take us through in order to get us to the land that He promised. Being in the desert is not easy. It is not a place of comfort, it is a dry place that is hot during the day and extremely cold during the night. The desert can be a place of drought but it can be the place in which we are nourished by God directly. You cannot appreciate the rain of blessings that will come unless you've experienced drought. The desert can be a place of confusion. It may be a place in which we wonder "where are you taking me God?". However, the desert might be the only place in which we are truly going to learn how to rely on God's direction. It is a place in which we can only find comfort in God's presence because there is no water or food available. The desert can be the place in which we feel the most vulnerable and yet safe because God Himself will be the one guiding us through it.

The desert can mean many things for many of us. It can bring many emotions, many mind traps.

A common thing that happens in the desert is to see a "mirage". A mirage is defined as "an optical illusion caused by an atmospheric condition". Through our deserts, we might see things come up that look like our promised land but when we look closely, they are not. This leaves us with disappointments and disbelief. We start doubting that the promised land even exists. However, we believe in a God of reality and not mirages. His promises are as real as the air that we breathe. We may not see the air, but we do not hesitate to breathe as we know that it is at our disposal.

We must learn to find comfort in God through our deserts. Yes, we may wonder, "where are you taking me?" but let that question turn into a bold statement that shouts "wherever you take me, I will go Lord". His promises are real, His promises shall come to pass. Don't heed to doubt, He who promised will be faithful to fulfill His promise.

## OVERCOME

To conclude, it is normal to experience doubt when time passess by and you do not see your promise fulfilled. There are choices that we can take when facing doubt. We can either dwell on it or learn to overcome it. God tells us in Isaiah 41:10 '*Do not fear, for I am with you; Do not anxiously look about you, for I am your God I will strengthen you, surely I will help you, Surely I will uphold you with My righteous right hand.*' He reassures us that He will be with us and strengthen us as we await for the promise.

One last thought, a promise does not necessarily die with an individual. While I was watching the Bible series on Netflix, I recalled one episode in which Moses tells the Israelites about his excitement of going to the promised land as they were going to fulfill Abraham's covenant. While I cannot say that Moses said this verbatim to the Israelites, it brought to remembrance that a promise does not die with an individual. The Abrahamic covenant was renewed with Isaac and then with Jacob (Gen. 26:3; Gen. 28:13-15). Though Abraham had ceased to exist in the world as we know it, his promise was going to be fulfilled through his generation.

When my former church, Heaven on Earth Church, lost its pastor on April 2, 2017, doubt started to creep in among many of us in the church. It was a totally unexpected event that many of us are still recovering from. Doubt made some people "jump ship" but a remnant was still there. This is not to say that the remnant didn't doubt but we had to garment ourselves with courage from the Lord to be able to continue the work our pastor had started. Just as the Israelites, we were going to fulfill the covenant that was made with Heaven on Earth.

There is hope for those who wait in Jesus. He who overcame the world gives us the courage to move forward despite the fear and doubt, despite not seeing things come to pass in the natural. Just wait.

# Chapter 3

# ISHMAELS

*"Then Sarai, Abram's wife, took Hagar her maid, the Egyptian, and gave her to her husband Abram to be his wife, after Abram had dwelt ten years in the land of Canaan. So he went in to Hagar, and she conceived. And when she saw that she had conceived, her mistress became despised in her eyes."*
Genesis 16:3-4

**"Doing things your way can give birth to an Ishmael when God destined you to give birth to an Isaac"**

The quote above is a word that God deposited in my heart as I was waiting for my promised son, Isaak. Towards the end of 2016, I had planned in meticulous detail how 2017 was going to go for me and my family. My husband was involved in the planning of course. While my plans were good and appeared to please the Lord, I did not factor Him completely into the equation. I wrote down deadlines for certain things, including having a baby. I remember that one of my goals for 2017 was to have a baby by December of that year. In retrospect, how foolish of me to add the creation of a human being to my list of goals! I laugh about it now but I can guarantee you that as I waited, desperation started to kick in.

While I did not take the same measures as Sarai, which was to offer my husband another wife so she could bear me a son, I did engage in certain patterns of thinking that were pessimistic and doubtful of the promise that God had given me. I started to think that if God didn't want to give me children it was ok and my husband and I even considered adoption as a future option. I still consider adoption as a future option but in the moment, I considered it as my "plan b" to fulfill my desire of being a mother. Through the quote that God deposited in my heart, I understood that all I needed to do was wait upon my promise because I would run the risk of messing things up if I decided to do things my way.

During my process, I learned to define what an "Ishmael" meant in my life. My definition of an "Ishmael" is *a carnal solution that attempts to replace a heavenly promise.* As a disclosure, this is not what the name Ishmael means. The name Ishmael actually means "God hears", which is a beautiful meaning in itself. For me, an Ishmael meant trying to find my own solution, doing things my way, trying to help God and taking Him out of the equation. You see, many times God gives us a word and we want to know the full process of how that word will come to pass. I have come to believe that if God revealed to us the full picture, we would mess it up at some point.

*"Then  God said to Abraham, "As for Sarai your wife, you shall not call her name Sarai, but Sarah shall be her name. And I will bless her and also give you a son by her; then I will bless her, and she shall be a mother of nations; kings of people shall be from her." Then Abraham fell on his face and laughed, and said in his heart, "Shall a child be born to a man who is one hundred years old? And shall Sarah, who is ninety years old, bear a child?" And Abraham said to God, "Oh, that Ishmael might live before you!" Then God said: "No, Sarah your wife shall bear you a son, and you shall call his name Isaac; I will establish my covenant with him for an everlasting covenant, and with his descendants after him. And as for Ishmael, I have heard you. Behold, I have blessed him, and will multiply him exceedingly. He shall beget twelve princes, and I will make him a great nation. But my covenant I will establish with Isaac, whom Sarah shall bear to you at this set time next year"* Genesis 17:15-21

God's covenants are not made with the Ishmaels we give birth to in the flesh but through the Isaacs that are birthed from God's heart. Abraham not only laughed at what God was telling him rather he tried to tell God how to fulfill His promise. We have all been at this point, haven't we? Trying to tell God how to do His job! Now, we see that Ishmael was blessed because of a promise that was made to

Abraham. This instance gives us a glimpse of hope and how merciful our God is. Even though Abraham took matters upon himself to fulfil a heavenly promise, God in His infinite mercy allowed Ishmael to enjoy some of the benefits of that promise. After all, it wasn't Ishmael's fault. God had to remind Abraham that the *covenant* was made with Isaac.

As stated before, God is not only a God of promises but He is a God of covenants. God is relational. A covenant is essentially an agreement between two or more parties to do or not to do something. A covenant can give birth to many promises within it. A covenant holds even greater weight than a promise as it involves having a relationship with the promising party rather than just being left with a simple promise of something being done. Yes, Ishmael was going to enjoy some of the benefits of the promise but God wanted to have a relationship with Isaac and his generation.

While God in His infinite mercy may allow your Ishmaels to be blessed, these situations created by ourselves can actually birth bondange upon our lives. Covenants of the flesh will birth bondage. The Bible gives a perfect comparison of the covenant that was born in the flesh, Ishmael, and the one that was born in the Spirit, Isaac on Galatians 4:21-31:

> **21** *Tell me, you who want to live under the law, do you know what the law actually says?* **22** *The Scriptures say that*

*Abraham had two sons, one from his slave wife and one from his freeborn wife.[a] 23 The son of the slave wife was born in a human attempt to bring about the fulfillment of God's promise. But the son of the freeborn wife was born as God's own fulfillment of his promise.*

*24 These two women serve as an illustration of God's two covenants. The first woman, Hagar, represents Mount Sinai where people received the law that enslaved them. 25 And now Jerusalem is just like Mount Sinai in Arabia,[b] because she and her children live in slavery to the law. 26 But the other woman, Sarah, represents the heavenly Jerusalem. She is the free woman, and she is our mother. 27 As Isaiah said, "Rejoice, O childless woman, you who have never given birth! Break into a joyful shout, you who have never been in labor! For the desolate woman now has more children  than the woman who lives with her husband!"[c]*

*28 And you, dear brothers and sisters, are children of the promise, just like Isaac. 29 But you are now being persecuted by those who want you to keep the law, just as Ishmael, the child born by human effort, persecuted Isaac, the child born by the power of the Spirit.*

*30 But what do the Scriptures say about that? "Get rid of the slave and her son, for the son of the slave woman will not share the inheritance with the free woman's son."[d] 31 So, dear brothers and sisters, we are not children of the slave woman; we are children of the free woman.*

The covenant that was born in the flesh, Ishmael, brought bondage to Abraham physically and spiritually. Abraham now was forced to deal with Hagar and Ishmael, which brought strife between him and Sarah.  In the same way, these covenants that are born of the flesh could bring emotional consequences, such as anxiety, depression, guilt, apathy, strife, anger and deprive us from enjoying the freedom of having a relationship with God. Shame can come into the picture and prevent us from fully going into the presence of the Lord due to the carnal decision we made. The devil will make a point to remind us of the desperate decision we made when God has already forgiven us for our desperation. Your Ishmael will make it a point to keep you in bondage when you are already free.

## "The end of a covenant of bondage will birth your journey to your promised land"

The minute we decide to leave Egypt (what kept us in bondage) behind, is the minute we can start walking into what God promises us. The covenants that are made through the Isaacs in our lives bring us freedom! Freedom to enjoy a relationship with God; making us children of the promise. Don't wallow on the mistake you might have made out of desperation. There is hope. God is infinite in grace and mercy. While we may not be fully absolved from the consequences of our actions, my God is a God of second chances! In Numbers 12:10-15, He gave Miriam a second chance by forgiving her for her rebellious spirit thus healing her from leprosy. He gave humanity a second chance after the flood by finding Noah righteous and preserving his life along with his family's. He gives us a second chance when we come to Him in repentance.

Ishmaels can reflect in the decisions we make, and as presented before, they can be well intended. They are those things that we do that seem logical to us. There are a few examples of Ishmaels or what could have turned to be Ishmaels in the Bible. For example, in 1 Samuel 24 we see that David spares Saul's life. To give you some background on David and Saul, Saul was anointed the first king of Israel but due to his disobedience, he is rejected as king. God uses the prophet Samuel to anoint David as the new king. Saul becomes aware of this eventually and engages in persecuting David with the purpose of killing him. During one of these persecution episodes, David finds himself in the same cave as Saul and he sneaks right behind him. It was the perfect opportunity to kill Saul. To anyone's mind, it would've made perfect sense to kill him, it would've been the "fair" thing to do being that Saul had attempted against David's life many times. However, David only cut off a corner of Saul's robe and his response was that he would not hurt the Lord's anointed.

When reading this, in our human mentality, we could have assumed a position of thinking that David was crazy for not killing Saul when he had the chance. Wouldn't it make sense to kill Saul and take over the kingdom, just as God had promised David he would? In what mind would a man spare the life of someone who had been trying to kill him? In David's mind. You see, David was a man after God's own heart and he understood that taking matters into his own hands could have created an "Ishmael" situation. David maintained his integrity even when he waited to receive what was ordained and righteously his according to the promise that the Lord was giving him. David knew to not bring a carnal solution to fulfill a heavenly promise. Even more, God will never be pleased with us taking a sinful action to fulfill His promises in our lives.

In your life, you may encounter situations in which you may be able to "fulfill God's promise" by force or by doing something that will make you lose your integrity. However, as children of God, we must respect the anointed and do things in righteousness, even when we know we are next in line and the position was promised to us.

I love to compare promises with the process of pregnancy. Not just because I am going through it myself as I write but because most promises involve a word that some of us cringe at: *process*. And what a long process! Pregnancy is usually 40 weeks, and sometimes even 42 weeks. Your Isaacs in life will come after you have gone through a process. During this process you may experience trials but they are all in preparation for the promise that is to come. In pregnancy, if you get ahead of the process you may wind up with a miscarriage, stillbirth or premature baby.

Do not allow the discomfort of the process make you take decisions that will be spiritually fatal. Many ministries, dreams and goals are dead today because of decisions made out of not wanting to go through a process. Many churches are closed today because individuals with Pastoral callings went ahead of their process and jumped right into ministry.

The enemy will come after your process because he knows that if you leave the process ahead of time, the promise will be forfeited. When we think of the word process, I also think of the word desert, as mentioned before. Jesus was in the desert for 40 days, fasting, when the enemy began tempting Him. What is peculiar about the way that the enemy tempted Jesus is that he threatened Jesus' identity by saying "if you are the son of God". It is important to be grounded in your identity, who God says you are, as you endeavor in your process because if you are not, you will compromise your pursuit of holiness just to prove who you are. Jesus didn't allow the enemy to win by refusing to engage in a behavior that was out of order, which the enemy was trying to use to disprove Jesus' identity. Jesus knew who He was, He didn't have to do anything to prove it. Satan continued by offering other things that would lead to a similar outcome, Jesus being exalted. Jesus would be exalted by man, yet not by God. Jesus understood that prior to Him being exalted by the One who really mattered, He had to go through pain, process and trials in order for it to be done according to God's will. The enemy will give you false promises just to get you to abort the process. Know who you are in Christ and remain in the process that God has led you to.

The Israelites spent 40 years in the desert prior to entering the promised land as preparation for their promised land. Not only was this a season of preparation for them but also a new generation needed to be born. Forty years in the desert, forty days in the desert, forty weeks in the womb. In the Bible, we can see the number forty repeated many times. I don't believe it is coincidence. This number marks a new beginning, a new cycle, a new generation. The wait may be prolonged yet it is birthing something new.

With the perspective the Israelites had while they were so close to the land, they would have not known how to obtain the victory and take the land that was promised to them. It was in the desert that the Israelites truly got to know their God. How can you know the God who can make water spring out of the driest desert if you have not been through the desert yourself?

As you wait for God's promise to be fulfilled in your life, you will get to know a different name of God. When Moses had the encounter with the burning bush in the desert, he was able to know God as the I AM. He didn't have to conform with just the God of Abraham, Isaac and Jacob, he was able to know God at a personal level. Just as God became a relational God to Abraham by making a covenant,

He became relational with Moses by showing him His *personal name*. Through your process, or your desert, God wants to have a personal and true encounter with you. He no longer wants you to know the God of your forefathers; He wants you to know Him personally.

Moses knew of God. Although he was raised with an Egyptian education, he was also raised by his Hebrew family. The process served to strip him from his Egyptian preconceptions and education in order to truly know the I AM. God will take you through a desert in order to show you the true essence of him. In order for this to happen, He will take you through a process to strip you from past points of view, perspectives and preconceptions that do not allow you to see God for who He truly is. Moses could now confidently say "I AM THAT I AM sent me" to Pharaoh because he had this encounter with God in the midst of his desert. Do not despise the desert. Do not rebuke the desert. It is necessary to prepare you for where God wants to take you; your promised land and your Isaac.

Just as the fulfillment of a promise affects your household, the Ishmaels we create also affect the generations to come. Historically, Ishmael's lineage can be traced to the Arab and Muslim generation. Thousands of years later, one man's decision has led to the Arab-Israeli conflict that has impacted the world itself. I am sure that Abraham and Sarah did not think of the massive consequences that their decision was going to have. It can be deemed impossible to truly see the magnitude of the consequences of our actions in future generations. This is why it is important to ask God for directions as we walk into the promise given.

## LAST BUT NOT LEAST

Something that I had forgotten is that God has a habit of depositing great purpose on the youngest! Isaac was the youngest, yet child of the promise. Jacob was the youngest, yet he was blessed. Joseph was one of the youngest yet he ruled over Egypt. Jacob crossed his hands and blessed Manasseh (the youngest) rather than Ephraim (the oldest). David was the youngest of his brothers and was anointed king. Being the youngest does not make you the least in the eyes of the Lord! The last shall be first and the first shall be last. Don't be so concerned with being first. Ishmael is not necessarily the child of the promise because he's the oldest. Just because you are last, you are not the least. Deuteronomy 28:13 says *"The LORD will make you the head, not the tail. If you pay attention to the commands of the LORD your God that I give you this day and carefully follow them, you will always be at the top, never at the bottom"*. When you walk in obedience, you may be last in chronological order but it does not make you the tail, you are the head. You may be the last under the standards of men, yet first under the standards of God.

There have been "Ishmaels" that I have made in my life out of impatience. They led me to settle for things that I clearly knew God did not have for me. The shame of those mistakes created a mind trap that led me to believe that "that was it", that I had to settle because it was what I deserved due to those mistakes. Despite my mistakes, I see God's infinite grace and mercy in full display on a daily basis. In my human mentality, I thought that I didn't deserve to have an amazing husband and start a brand new family but every day I hear the whisper of God's voice telling me "I know the plans I have for you, plans of peace; plans of goodness" (Jeremiah 29:11). God truly has turned my ashes into beauty and He can do it with you as well. God's plan is not to bring condemnation upon these mistakes but forgiveness and bring us freedom from making the same mistakes. Don't allow the same Ishmaels to take root in your life but take the opportunity of a brand new day to truly walk in the will of God. You are on your way to your promise, don't let desperation or shame stop you from getting there.

# Chapter 4

# COVENANT REMINDERS

*"After these things the word of the Lord came to Abram in a vision, saying "Do not be afraid, Abram. I am your shield, your exceedingly great reward." But Abram said, "Lord God, what will you give me, seeing I go childless, and the heir of my house is Eliezer of Damascus?" Then Abram said, "Look, you have given me no offspring; indeed one born in my house is my heir! And behold, the word of the Lord came to him saying, "This one shall not be your heir, but one who will come from your own body shall be your heir". Then He brought him outside and said, "Look now toward heaven, and count the stars if you are able to number them." And He said to him, "So shall your descendants be." And he believed in the Lord, and He accounted it to him for righteousness."*
Genesis 15: 1-6

Just like Abraham needed a reminder of the promises made, we need those daily reminders as well. Something that does catch my attention of Genesis 15 is that at the end of the chapter, we see that God makes a *covenant* with Abraham. In Genesis 12 is when we first see the *promises* made to Abraham but then in Genesis 15 such promises are solidified into a *covenant*. As I have written before, God did not just give us promises but He has made a covenant with us for He is a relational God. God is not satisfied with just completing His end of the bargain but He wants to continue to have a relationship with us even after such promises have been fulfilled.

God had to give a reminder of His promise to Abraham approximately 11 years after he was first given the promise of having offspring. In his humanity, it is logical for Abraham to engage in doubt. After all, his present situation contradicted the word that God had deposited within him. As children of God, we will go through situations that are completely the opposite of what God has promised us. It was in one of those moments in which God brought Abraham out of his tent in order to give him an illustration of the magnitude of His promise. Abraham needed to get out of his present situation, from his tent, in order to see what God wanted him to see and truly understand the promise that God was giving him. Even if your situation seems contrary to what God told you, ask him to bring you out of your tent in order to remind you of His promise. The tent can represent many things. It could be your very own mindset. Ask the Lord to renew your mind, to see what He sees, hear what He hears and declare the word that He has spoken over your life.

It is time to break thinking patterns, habits and behaviors that keep us stuck in our human vision and do not allow us to see the magnitude of the promise. Abraham was led outside of his tent but he had to take the step to get out. He had to see the stars in the midst of the darkest night in order to truly understand what God was promising him.

## A SIGN OF THE COVENANT

There are certain things that God does or that we have to do in order to be reminded of the covenant that has been made with Him. The Bible gives us a few examples of representations of reminders of covenants. Whatever that means for you, it is important for us to remember the promises that God made us but also the covenant that has been made.

On one occasion, I went to my mom's house and we were trying to feel for my son moving inside my womb. I told her he wasn't kicking at the moment and said to me "but he moves right?" And I said "of course!" I didn't catch this revelation at that moment but later on, that night, I ended up wide awake at 1am and I started feeling for my baby's kicks. I suddenly started to have an apprehension about him being alive and well inside of me. Suddenly God's word came to me and told me "The promise is alive within you even when you or others don't feel it moving at the moment". Wow! I couldn't believe the simplicity and yet the depth of those words. God reminded me that Isaak was my promised child and even when he wasn't kicking, he was alive and well.

God's promises for you will not always be creating a full manifestation in your life. Yet, you must always remember the promise that has been deposited within you. There is a promise within you that is alive and well, even when you feel it's "dormant". Just like a pregnancy, you may not see your belly showing yet but something is happening in your womb. Your promise may not be visible to others but no one in this world can tell you that is not alive just because they can't see it.

If you need a reminder of your promise, do ask God for something to stir up within you to remember His promise for you. A few minutes after that word was deposited within me, my son started to kick up a storm! I see his movements as God always reminding me of His promise. His kicks were a brief manifestation and reminder of God's promise.

God will allow some manifestations of the promise to feed your faith but He will also allow the quiet moments for you to place your faith in Him and not in the promise. In Genesis 22, God asks Abraham to offer Isaac as a sacrifice of burnt offering. I can only imagine the pain yet peace that Abraham's soul must have experienced at that moment. I personally would have asked God so many questions. However, the Word says that the next day, Abraham got up and headed to make the sacrifice asked from him. As the story progresses, he decides to leave his servants behind and tells them *"the boy and I will travel a little farther. We will worship there, and then we will come right back"* (New Living Translation). What a level of faith! God had just asked him for his son yet Abraham is telling his servant *"WE* will be right back". Abraham was so certain of the promise that was given to him that he made a declaration even when God was clearly asking him to sacrifice his son. Even when his son would ask him about where the sacrifice was, he would say that God would provide it. Abraham continues with the task required and picks up his knife to complete the sacrifice. This is what I call a quiet moment. It is that crucial moment in which your faith is tested. Isaac was the living manifestation of God's promise in Abraham's life but that brief moment in between the time that Abraham picked up his knife and the Angel of the Lord spoke to him was that quiet moment. It was in that quiet moment in which Abraham's faith was truly tested and he placed it back on God.

The quiet moment can be a time in which God may not be clearly speaking to you yet He is asking you to go forth in obedience. These are the moments in which you place your faith in the God who promised! These are key moments that capture the true essence of faith, which is being certain and convinced of what is hoped for even when your eyes see the opposite. Abraham could have thought that his promise would end there but his promise was just getting started. Isaac was just a small manifestation of the true magnitude of God's promise for Abraham and his household. The Word says that after Abraham made the sacrifice provided by God, God once again promises Abraham many descendants. This time they were not just going to be as countless as the stars in the heavens but they would also be as countless as the sand on the seashore. Not only he was going to be blessed but all the nations of the earth would be blessed as well. After Sarah's death, God gave Abraham many more sons, making an even greater manifestation of his promise.

In those quiet moments, in those moments in which your promise is not "moving" or seems lifeless, always remember that they are the perfect opportunity to place your faith once again in the God who promised. The promise is still alive and well within you. It is not about to end, is just starting. When your marriage seems like it's about to end, declare that it is just getting started. When your children seem hopelessly lost, declare that they are men and women of God. When your finances are about to drain out, declare provision over your household. Make a bold statement, place your faith back in the Promise Maker.

While physical reminders of your promise are important, they are not what qualify you as a person of faith. Take Abraham as an example. The word says in Romans 4:10 that Abraham was counted as righteous because of his faith prior of his circumcision. This act was just a physical reminder of the circumcision that had already happened in his heart by placing his faith in a God of Covenants. I encourage you to take a moment right now, make a pause from reading this book and read Romans Chapter 4. Take some time to truly understand what this chapter is speaking to your life. Write what it means for you. After you are done, come back to reading this chapter. God's promise for Abraham was not based on mere works of obedience but in the relationship that he had with God. Abraham was counted as righteous not because he was about to sacrifice his son of the promise rather he was counted as righteous from the moment that he decided to go forth with what God was asking from him.

Signs of a covenant can come in many different shapes or forms. Abraham was asked to be circumcised along with each male among his household and future generations. This was a physical reminder of the covenant that God made with him. However, going back to Romans 4, this physical reminder is not what counted towards Abraham's righteousness rather it was the mark that Abraham's faith had left in his heart.

According to sources and history[2], due to the threat of Greek paganism, circumcision became a distinction of fidelity to a covenant. It was what distinguished children of

_______________

[2] https://www.biblestudytools.com/dictionary/circumcision/

the Covenant from the Gentiles. However, it was not this physical act that brought salvation rather it was the spiritual fidelity that individuals had to a covenant established with God.  How I see this physical sign of a covenant is as an outward manifestation of the spiritual sign that was imprinted in Abraham's heart. When you are completely sold out to Jesus, when you are committed to walking a path of righteousness, your outward life will be a physical manifestation of the circumcision of your heart. Allow for the circumcision of your heart to be a daily reminder of the covenant that God has made with you. Following Christ is more a matter of the heart than a matter of behavior. Why? Because someone can be externally circumcised yet not have a covenant with God.

Wear a sign of the covenant over your heart, but if you need a physical representation of this reminder do so as well. As I think of signs of the covenant, I think of how a married couple wears a ring on their left ring finger as a symbol of their union. It is not just to remind themselves of the covenant, as we know that that reminder should be already imprinted in their hearts, rather it is to remind others of the covenant that has been made between each other. Wear a sign that reminds the devil that you have made a covenant with God. He will try to stir you astray from your journey to your promise, from your covenant with God. After all, that is what he did in the Garden of Eden. His sole purpose is to destroy the relationship between God and us. However, a physical representation, your worship, your declaration, can remind him that you have made a covenant with the Faithful one. No matter the darts that he will try to send your way, you can always remind him and yourself of your covenant.

One of my favorite songs is "You won't relent" by Jesus Culture. The song is an adaptation of Songs of Solomon 8:6 and it says "I'll set you as a seal upon my heart, as a seal upon my arm. For there is love, that is as strong as death, jealousy demanding as the grave. And many waters cannot quench this love". That is my prayer to God. I will set my sign of the covenant in my heart, where only Him and I can see, and on my arm, where others can see that I belong to Him. His love for us, His faithfulness and commitment to us, His bride, cannot be drowned by the raging waves of the storm.

## A NEW NAME

> *5 No longer shall your name be called Abram, but your name shall be Abraham; for I have made you a father of many nations.* Genesis 17:5

> *15 Then God said to Abraham, "As for Sarai your wife, you shall not call her name Sarai, but Sarah shall be her name. 16 And I will bless her and also give you a son by her; then I will bless her, and she shall be a mother of nations; kings of peoples shall be from her."* Genesis 17: 15-16

Not only was Abraham asked to become circumcised as a

sign of the covenant but God changes his name. Originally, Abram means "exalted father". However, God's new name for him gave him new purpose, now being named "father of many nations". Abraham was marked for fatherhood since his birth based on his given name. God's purpose for his life went beyond the name that he was given at birth. The verse that comes to mind as I think of this name change is Ephesians 3:20. God will do infinitely more than what we asked for. Abraham's original name limited him to human-given purpose yet God wants your name to match his God-given purpose for your life.

Sarai went from being "quarrelsome", the meaning of Sarai, to "princess", the meaning of Sarah. They both had not seen the promise be fulfilled yet but their names were already changed. When God gives you a new name, He gives you a new identity. Our identity no longer rests on our current circumstances rather on who God says we are. Once God has given us a new identity, we must walk as such. God changes your name from wife to mother, from husband to father, from single woman to married woman, from unemployed to entrepreneur, etc. Stop walking according to your own name and walk according to your new identity in Christ.

God changed Abraham's and Sarah's name, just as a bride changes her name when she makes a covenant with her bridegroom. Such change signifies the unification of both parties in an unbreakable covenant. One of the strongest tactics that the enemy will try to use to destroy our relationship with God is to confuse our identity and our perception of who God truly is. There are bondages and sins that could seem greater to overcome because they go to the core of who were are; our identity. The serpent, through trickery, led Eve to doubt the words that God had spoken over her and Adam. He provided a twarthed perspective of who God was by making God seem as a selfish God by not wanting them to eat from the tree of knowledge of good and evil.

The enemy will try to lead you to believe that God is unfaithful to His covenant and that He has forgotten about you. I sure have felt that way. Satan, as the father of lies, will attempt to damage the image of God because if he succeeds, he will damage your self-image. Think about it. We were created in the image and likeness of God. I have discovered that many of us tend to walk defeated and with low self-esteem because we fail to look at ourselves in the same way that God looks at us, which is in His image and likeness. No, we are not perfect like God, we do not possess all of His attributes as we are merely human. However, God, as our Creator, as Our Father, can give us an accurate picture of who we are or supposed to be.

You may be wondering, how does a name change relate to identity? It is the American custom for a bride to change her last name to her husband's once they get married, as stated before. Names carry a lot of weight into what makes us, *us*. When a woman changes her last name to her husband's upon marriage, she's making a public statement of the covenant that she made. She went from "single woman" to "married woman". This changes how she views herself and how others in turn see her. Do not misinterpret me, there is nothing wrong with not changing your last name to your husband's. This is a cultural practice that represents an external sign of a covenant. Some women see this practice as losing their identity. However, I see it as an external manifestation of an internal transformation. In the same way, God changed Abraham and Sarai's names as a manifestation of the promise and covenant that He had made with them. This name change gave them a new identity; not a man-given identity but a God-given one.

With all of this being said, when the enemy tries to call you by a different name, you have to remind him of the identity that has been given to you by God Himself. Do not respond by any other name. Remind him that your covenant, your name change, makes you one with God. If he tries to call you lost, remind him you are found. If he tries to call you rejected, remind him you are accepted. If he tries to call you worthless and unloved, remind him you are valued and loved by the God of Covenants.

## A NEW PERSPECTIVE

As I think of assuming a new perspective, I can't help but think of Joshua and Caleb. Joshua and Caleb were two of the twelve spies who were sent on a quest to explore the Promised Land. Their story can be found in Numbers 13. When the spies returned, they were able to report the good things of the land. However, they added a "but" at the end of their report. How many times do we find ourselves adding "buts" at the end of the promises of God? We say, God promised me a job, but… God promised me a husband but… God promised me a child but… God promised me a ministry but… We can think of many reasons why the promises will not be fulfilled! We are able to recognize the goodness of the promises but then we place many excuses as to why we cannot move forward towards them.

The Bible says in Number 13: 30 that Caleb quieted the people and encouraged them to go and conquer for "we are well able to overcome it". We must assume a "Joshua and Caleb Perspective", a point of view that allows us to see beyond the giants and gives us the courage to go conquer the land that God has promised us. As I had shared before, there were a few instances in which other "spies" pointed out the giants as I walked to my promise. I even started to point out the giants myself and started to engage in a thinking pattern of disbelief. I do praise God that the thoughts were just passing thoughts and I did not allow for them to overtake my mind and my heart. I do not think I would be writing this book if they would have overtaken me. I cannot lie, seeing others have *my* promise fulfilled in their lives was a little sad. I started to feel like I was left behind. However, how was God going to fulfill His promise at that time if I didn't even believe it myself? I had to change my perspective. I had to stop seeing the giants in front of my promise and focus on the milk and honey. As I thought of this statement, I was reminded of the song called "Fall" by Belonging Co. Meditate on the lyrics of this song, if you can, look it up and just let those words sink into your spirit. We all need a reminder to change our perspectives.

**//My eyes above what it looks like//**
**I will only see all You promised me**
**//My eyes above what it looks like//**
**I want what You want, I want Kingdom come**

**//Let the weight of Heaven//**
**///Fall///**
**//Have Your way//**

**//My faith beyond what it feels like//**
**All the way to You**
**All the way to breakthrough, breakthrough**
**//My faith beyond what it feels like//**
**Not by power or might**
**Holy Spirit right now**

**Something's changing in the spirit**
**Something's breaking, I can feel it**
**Heaven come down, heaven come down**[3]

---

[3] https://genius.com/The-belonging-co-fall-lyrics

Place your eyes above what your current situation looks like. There's a reason we look above. When we set our eyes on the things above, we can learn to see things from God's perspective. When you learn to want "Kingdom Come", you are satisfied with God's desires for your life. Therefore; every promise is fulfilled. Believe that something is changing, declare that the chains that were holding you are breaking. Despite not seeing them broken yet, something is happening. Something is shifting in the heavenly realm.

Are we going to be conformed with eating manna in the desert when God has a promised land full of milk and honey? The Lord had promised this land to Abraham and the Israelites were the rightful heirs to it. Yet, they allowed for their doubt and lack of faith to get in the way of what was rightfully theirs. Do not ignore the giants, pray for God to give you strategies on how to defeat them so you can go and conquer what is rightfully yours.

The people of Israel were almost at the promised land when they sent the spies but they based their ability to conquer on a negative report of the majority. Pastor Gideon Mba stated during one preaching at my former church that God is not looking for a majority, He is looking for a remnant. Caleb and Joshua were that remnant. A remnant is not defined by numbers, it is defined by those who hold on the word of God despite what their eyes are seeing. Caleb and Joshua saw the promise for what it actually was.

The promise is fixed, you just have to walk and conquer.

## WRITTEN PROMISES

In the times of Israel, a promise or any arrangement was taken legally serious just as it was spoken. It did not have to be written into a legal document for it to be valid. This is why in Genesis 27 we see that Isaac was not able to give another verbal blessing to Esau as it was already given to Jacob. A man's word alone held authority. While spoken promises hold authority, I have found that writing our promises hold even more power. The Bible itself is proof of the impact that reading a promise over and over again can have upon our lives.

I have a habit and I encourage you to write every single word the Lord has given you. I have a drawing of my son's name, before I even became pregnant and around the drawing I wrote every single promise that God had given me in relation to him. Every time that I would get discouraged or desperate, I would look at that page and my strength would be renewed. I used that page as a reference to pray. I would pray that God would continue to remind me of His promise. I would speak to the voices of discouragement by reflecting back on what was written.

Writing your promises on a journal is important but an additional step I took in journaling was writing the resolution of that promise and when it was fulfilled. This book was born out of my habit of writing my experiences with the Lord. It is always a great experience to look back at my journals and just reflect on how good and faithful the Lord has been. Believe me, the writing will serve as a reminder. Sometimes it is easy to look at the storms in life and lose track of who God is. He never stops being who He is, we just forget. Having these written experiences can give us a map when we lose our sense of direction.

## WALK IN OBEDIENCE

The greatest way to honor the covenant with the Lord is walking in obedience. The Lord told Abraham in Genesis 17:1-3 to walk before Him and be 'blameless". If you are anything like me, blind obedience is difficult. The minute you give me a command, I would like to know what is the outcome of that command. I would like to know why you are asking me to do it. I can't lie, a few years back, if God would have told me to "pick up and leave to the land I will show you" just like He did to Abraham, I would've replied "but where is this land exactly?" The problem with this mentality, with wanting to know the outcome, is that you miss out on the surprises that God has for your life as you engage on the journey. You have set expectations that you have created in your limited mind, when the Unlimited God has things far greater than you can imagine for your life (Ephesians 3:20). Our limitations just create anxiety and stress over things that we do not know for sure will happen. Our negative outlook on life just places a limit on what God can actually do. I believe that many times we cut ourselves short from many blessings because of living in a state of unbelief.

It is normal to doubt at times. After all, we are only human. I was impacted by a preaching by Pastor Steven Furtick in which he mentioned that faith is not the absence of doubt rather it is the mechanism to break through it. As you walk in obedience, you will question certain steps that the Lord is asking you to take. I remember desiring in my heart to have a bigger office for my counseling practice and as soon as the office that I wanted would become available, I would become doubtful of how I was going to afford it. Through these experiences, the Lord had to confront me lovingly and tell me "My child, wasn't this what you were asking for? Just walk, the doors are wide open". I didn't need to worry about the outcome, or how I was going to provide. My God was going to do the rest, for I knew that if He called me, He was going to provide.

# Chapter 5

# PATIENTLY WAITING

*And so after waiting patiently, Abraham received what was promised.* Hebrews 6:15

Waiting is not my strong suit. I have been like that since I was a child. Growing up I remember that computers had Windows 95 installed. I grew up in the era of "dial up" internet and having to limit web browsing time as it would make the land lines busy. No wifi, no high speed internet, no Netflix. Yet, my brain operated like many Millenials' brains work. One particular memory is me trying to make my computer work by constantly clicking the mouse. I was not conformed with a web page taking a whole two minutes to load. It felt like an eternity at the time. While I was clicking and clicking the mouse, I remember my father telling me "stop clicking so fast, you are going to freeze the computer". I think about it now and I laugh but 7 year old me thought that the more I clicked, the faster the computer would work. Don't we all engage in this behavior sometimes? We think that the more we rush someone, the faster they will tend to our needs. Even worse, we tend to think that the more we pray about something or the more we rush God, the faster He will respond to our needs. Ouch!

I prayed almost on a daily basis. I would become intimate with my husband like clockwork in order to make the pregnancy happen. Statistically, I thought "the more I do something, the faster I will get my results".  After all, we grew up with the mentality that "practice makes perfect" and "work hard and you will obtain everything you want". Nope.

I had to learn to savor the process while waiting for my promise to be fulfilled. Sometimes we are caught up in obtaining our outcome that we neglect to learn important lessons only thought by the process. God was allowing me to develop the heart of a mother before I became one. He was teaching me patience, balance, persistence, to seek Him for the sake of being intimate with Him rather than to obtain something from Him.

Abraham received his promise. We know that. But he had to patiently wait for it. Not desperately wait. When he "desperately waited", he received an Ishmael. When he "patiently waited", he received an Isaac. Colossians 3:12 encourages us to "clothe [our]selves with compassion, kindness, humility, gentleness and *patience*". I picture this as taking the "cloak" of patience everyday and being intentional about using it in every situation that presents. Believe me, when you commit to wanting to show the fruit of the Spirit, God will place you in situations that will test the fruit.

## WE ARE NOT LEFT BEHIND

There are times as we patiently wait, that we will feel left behind; sometimes even left behind by God. We see everyone around us getting that which we desire the most. We are doing things "the right way", we are even moving according to God's instructions but we just don't get our heart's desire. Those desires that you know were born out of God's own heart. It's rough. The feeling of being left out it's rough. However, the Bible says to take delight in the Lord and He will grant the desires of your heart.

In the midst of desperation, in the midst of feeling left behind, all God wants us to do is to take delight in Him. Is it easy? Not always. Taking delight in God even though you have not received your promise is never easy. It can even feel impossible. We cry. We feel pain because we don't see the promise fulfilled yet. God has spoken over and over again but we don't see the promise come to pass just yet. We see our own promise being fulfilled in other people's lives. Are we happy for that? Yes! We rejoice when other people are blessed and God is fulfilling His promises. But even then, disbelief slowly creeps in, disappointment attempts to make way into our hearts and we still feel like we are left behind.

There is a short phrase that God whispered into my ear when I felt like this. He said "You are not left behind". God himself reminded me that He is still thinking about me, He still sees the desire of my heart; He has not forgotten about me. God knows the most intimate desires of His daughters' and sons' hearts. He knows our deepest most secret longings. Those things that we haven't even shared or even spoken out loud have already been heard by our Creator's ears.

God whispers "I will give you more than you can even imagine", "I am not done with you, you just have to go through this season to know a different facet of me". The Word says that He who promised is faithful to fulfill His promise and He who started the good work shall be faithful to complete it. Maybe we don't see it yet. Maybe we can't visualize the promise yet but it's coming. It is coming. Just wait a little longer. Just take delight in God's presence while you wait.

## WAITING IS NOT ALWAYS LACK OF ACTION

*For the vision is yet for an appointed time; But at the end it will speak, and it will not lie. Though it tarries, wait for it; Because it will surely come, It will not tarry.* Habakkuk 2:3

Many times we take for granted Old Testament writings. I was very impacted by this verse as I realized that God will give us visions that are not for this time. The problem is that we want things now. There are promises that are for now, most are for later. This verse describes that the vision appointed by God will be fulfilled in the end. Even if it seems slow in coming, wait patiently, for it will surely take place. It will not be delayed.

As we wait for our promises, we get ready for them. We await with expectation rather than with hopelessness and discouragement. We get ready with the certainty that the promise will come to pass. We get ready with diligence. This premise takes me back to when my husband and I used to date. I would get diligently ready as I waited for him to get me. Yes, sometimes He would be delayed, but him coming to get me was always worth it. As I got ready for his arrival, I never got discouraged or ever thought that he would stand me up or leave me hanging. I trusted that he loved me enough, that he was committed enough to come get me at some point, even when I thought he was going to get me at 7pm and he actually showed at 7:30pm (true story). If I trusted my husband this much, being merely human, how much more should I trust my Heavenly Father? God is committed to you enough, He loves you enough to fulfill His promise in your life. Not just that, God will not fail to His own character. All you have to do is diligently get ready for such promise. Getting ready might mean different things for each person.

As I am writing this portion, I am 38 weeks pregnant. I am diligently getting ready for the arrival of my Isaak. I am not going to lie, I just can't wait until he arrives. However, I am just letting God do what He needs to do.  A sister from church even thought that my due date was delayed because my other two friends had given birth already! I told her, "no, I am not delayed, I am actually on time, they just happened to get ahead of their due date". It is interesting, because to an outsider's perspective, your promise may seem delayed but God's timing is perfect. Your promise is not delayed, other people just finished their process or their waiting time before you and their promise arrived sooner than yours. Continue to get ready diligently as you await your promise; it is not delayed, it is on time, on God's perfect time.

God taught me so much through the last few weeks of pregnancy. As I waited for Isaak to come, it started to seem as though those around me were getting more impatient than me to meet my son. I know that they loved him so much that they each wanted to meet him. But with this anticipation, I started to get many well intended suggestions on how to provoke Isaak's birth. The list was countless. I did almost all of them but by 39 weeks and 3 days, there was little progress in my body getting ready for birth. This is when I said "I'm done trying to provoke labor on my own, he will come when God wants to". From that day forward, my attitude changed and that's the answer I would give to everyone who would give me a well intended advice.

I am not sure if I have written this already but it's worth repeating. As children of God, we need to learn how to trust God and just wait in our process. There is nothing wrong with carrying a baby until 40 weeks yet those around me started to perhaps perceive like my promise wasn't coming on time because of something I was not doing, when it was something that the Lord needed to do, not me. We need to stop attributing to ourselves tasks that belong to God alone! The promise will come in God's time, as long as you continue walking in obedience. At the moment of my labor, God was not calling me to do things on my own to provoke it, He just wanted me to wait in Him, wait for His timing.

The promise is already within you. My promised son was resting comfortably within me but I was the one who was uncomfortable. The pain was real, the discomfort would feel eternal. I felt contractions all day long but never frequent enough to rush to the hospital. That's how your process will feel at times. Instead of focusing on the discomfort, await with expectation and rejoice for what you are carrying within you. The pain will be worth it. The discomfort will be worth it.

## THINGS YOU CAN CONTROL VERSUS THINGS YOU CAN'T

There are things that you just cannot control. We cannot get aggravated over these things or situations as we await for the promise. As I was saying earlier, in my process of labor, I could not control how quick I could give birth. Feelings of frustration would arise as time would pass and I could not do anything for my son to be born. I was reminded through this process that there are things that I cannot control, there are factors and variables that I cannot predict. When this happens,we just have to learn to accept them and allow the Holy Spirit to give us peace as we wait. The illusion of control ends up leaving us in a state of constant angst, always thinking about the future and missing out on the present.

As humans, emotions of desperation and despair would creep in. I allowed myself to feel these emotions at the moment because after all, God created us to be emotional beings. My feelings were not validated at times, I was told to "stay calm" constantly, which in all honesty created the opposite effect. The only one who could truly bring peace as I was in a "helpless situation" was God Himself. I casted my feelings and my thoughts on to the Lord, as 1 Peter 5:7 says.

Do not allow yourself to feel guilty over the feelings that will arise as a result of things that you cannot control. You may have to allow yourself to experience those feelings for a brief period of time and then soak yourself in the word of God. Allow His peace to help you as you wait. I personally love to be in control. From a human point of view, being in control has helped me succeed in many ways. However, I do embrace the fact that I cannot control everything because it means that the Almighty God Himself is the one who has control. From a psychological standpoint, it can be nerve wrecking to allow someone else to have control. As children of God, we can take comfort on the premise that God takes care of us. His ways are higher, His thoughts are higher, His plans are far better than the plans we have for our own lives.

You see, I had an agenda. I had plans for when I was "supposed to get pregnant" and unconsciously, I had plans for when I had to give birth. I had to let go of my own agenda and embrace God's agenda for my life. I gave birth at 40 weeks and three days. After the waiting, complications started to arise after my due date. My body was not reacting the way that it was "supposed to" in regards to labor, my blood pressure started to increase, putting us at risk. I went to the hospital expecting to have a baby in the "natural way" and ended up with a c-section. The recovery process was difficult. I longed to move freely to take care of my baby but I constantly had to depend on my family members to move around and do some of the most basic functions. I was in a journey of "dependency". I was not only being taught by God to depend on Him but

He was also teaching me to rely on my support system, the people He had placed around me.

After my complicated labor, I was diagnosed with postpartum preeclampsia, which led to high blood pressures that were out of my control. It was yet another hospitalization a week after giving birth and I had to leave my baby with family members while I was in the hospital. I felt powerless. I had to entrust my promised baby to others while I was being processed.

From March 6, 2018 through March 16, 2018, I had been poked on both arms multiple times, been poked on my back, tossed and turned and was cut open, just to sum it up. As I meditated on all of these things, I realized that these are my battle scars. These will be the scars that share the story of how God is glorifying Himself through my process. These scars are my testimony. If that is so, they are worth it. Painful, but worth it. These scars remind me of my promised child, my Isaak. He is worth it. You might get a few scars along the way as you walk into the promise but they ultimately glorify God. They ultimately show what God did in your life, they remind you and others of God's faithfulness.

There were physical scars due to my health complications that also left emotional scars. Anxiety is real. Sadness for "no reason" is real. Perinatal Mood Disorders are real. It is not just hormones. Some days I felt like I was falling apart and had no choice but to keep it together. Church, ministry, business and family issues were taking a toll on me, physically and emotionally. Many of you are just finding this out about me as you read this. The Counselor, the Church Leader, the one who led the congregation to worship from time, the one who translated for Pastor, the Preacher who was called to be a Pastor was falling apart and she had to keep it together. At least that's what I felt like at the time.

When you receive a promise, people expect you to be in a state of constant joy and wellness. It seems to others that all of your problems are solved because you received what you were waiting for. I thought that once I had my son the process would be over, but it was actually the beginning. I couldn't understand why I finally had my son yet I would burst into tears out of nowhere. I couldn't understand why just hearing him cry while changing his diaper would make me feel so anxious. I couldn't understand why despite eating healthy, getting rest, being medication compliant and taking things easy, my blood pressure wouldn't stabilize. Through it all though, one thing I learned; I am not in control. God is Sovereign, I am not. There are things that I can control yet they are things that I can't.

The promised land did not come easy to the people of Israel. It was at their disposition but the Israelites still needed to fight for it because there were things around it that presented as obstacles in order for them to make it where God wanted to take them. There were private battles I needed to fight in order to truly enjoy my promise, my son. Even after reaching the promised land, people forget that now you have to plow that land, you have to nourish it, all in contrast to when you were in the desert in which all your needs were provided by the Father. Yes, the Lord will continue to provide in the promised land, but the process should've taught you something, the process should've taken you to a deeper level. It is because of the deeper level that the process should've taken you to, that the expectation is higher, the price is higher and now rather than receiving manna from heaven, you have to plow the land in order to provide your nourishment. Now you have to work for the nourishment, for your daily bread. This does not mean that blessings constantly come due to our works, they come by grace. This means that you cannot take the promised land for granted. This means that there is a price that comes with the greatness of that blessing. It means that there are unique challenges that will come with the promised land but now you are able to face as you went through your desert. Many think that they get their promises and just get to relax and be in a state of pure joy and happiness. The promise is not the end, it's the beginning.

There was a moment as I was writing this book that I encountered a "writer's block". This took me by surprise as everything I write I hear clearly through the Holy Spirit. However, God showed me that I needed to go through a few more processes in order to finish my testimony, in order to walk with the promise.

Sarah was still faced with having to raise a child in her 90s. She was still faced on a daily basis with the fact that her husband had a child out of "wedlock", due to her influence, and was now creating problems in her family. She experienced unique challenges that she had to face, some because of her desperation but some that naturally came with her situation. Despite the challenges, we must continue to work the land, we must continue to raise that child, we must continue relying on God for strength in order for our promise to be a blessing to others.

*It was by faith that even Sarah was able to have a child, though she was barren and was too old. She believed[a] that God would keep his promise.* Hebrews 11:11

The word says in Hebrews 11:11 that by faith Sarah received strength to conceive and bore child past age. She needed to receive strength as she was weak. She was past age to this world's standards, she was as good as dead. When the world sees you as "past age" or as good as dead, remind them that God's promise comes to pass despite people's timelines, assumptions or agendas.

Patience is a fruit of the spirit but we can garment ourselves with it too (Colossians 3:12). Because it is a fruit, we need to allow the spirit to nourish it and always wait for it to blossom. Patience does not come naturally for many of us.

It sure doesn't come naturally to me. Your promise will teach you patience and it will bear the Spirit's fruit upon your life. This is why I love how Paul encourages us to garment ourselves with patience in Colossians 3:12. I see patience as this coat that I have to put on every day in order to challenge the thoughts of desperation and doubt. I must not only desire patience but embrace it and clothe myself with it on a daily basis.

## WAIT TILL TOMORROW

The phrase "you have to wait until tomorrow" is one of the phrases I dislike the most. In Spanish we have a saying, "no dejes para mañana lo que esta pa' hoy" or "don't leave for tomorrow what you can do today". I have always lived by those words; therefore, I am a very proactive person. I don't like to waste time. Procrastination is not part of my life. I was the type to have a paper ready one week before its due date when I was in college. You don't have to push me to get things done. Tomorrow is never promised so I try to do things today.

I realized why I do not like this phrase. It is because most of the time, when someone says "wait until tomorrow" it means that things are outside of my control. I start thinking of the possible scenarios that could happen between today and tomorrow. I start thinking that things will not come out as expected between today and tomorrow. Recently I went through an experience in which "wait until tomorrow" actually turned into "wait until next week". How debilitating was asking each day and getting the same answer!

Control… Oh how I love thee! I am transparent when it comes to this. I do love control but have come to accept that I do not have it. The more I want it, the more I lose it. Why? Because it is not mine to begin with. God is Sovereign, I am not. The Bible declares in Isaiah 55: 8-11:

> *For my thoughts are not your thoughts, neither are your ways my ways, declares the Lord. For as the heavens are higher than the earth, so are my ways higher than your ways and my thoughts than your thoughts. "For as the rain and the snow come down from heaven and do not return there but water the earth, making it bring forth and sprout, giving seed to the sower and bread to the eater, so shall my word be that goes out from my mouth; it shall not return to me empty, but it shall accomplish that which I purpose, and shall succeed in the thing for which I sent it.*

His ways are higher. His thoughts are higher. His plan is greater. My need for control only messes things up and gets me in situations that are more complicated than they should. I have come to realize that "wait till tomorrow" can actually yield to much greater things. "Wait till tomorrow" can make the difference between life and death. One day makes a difference. One day can make a difference between a fruit being ripe or green. One day can make a difference between a baby being full term or premature.

One day could make a difference between your promise turning to a blessing or a curse.

I have come to the realization that "wait till tomorrow" is God's gift for me to learn to trust in Him. One thing I can trust in and it is that God's word, His plan for my life, will not return to Him void. It is ok to be at a standstill because God is bringing His purpose to completion as I wait.

> *He says, "Be still, and know that I am God;  I will be exalted among the nations,   I will be exalted in the earth." Psalms 46:10*

## REST

> *On the seventh day God had finished his work of creation, so he rested[a] from all his work. Genesis 2:2*

Another key point of waiting is resting as you wait. Learn to rest in God. You do not have to worry about the outcome, just dwell in God's rest as you walk into your promise. God Himself gave us a perfect example of resting. He did not rest because He was tired rather He wanted to show us the beautiful gift of resting. Resting means different things for many. One definition of rest is to "cease work or movement in order to relax, refresh oneself, or recover strength."[4] One thing that caught my curiosity when looking for this particular definition of the word rest, is that

---

[4] www.dictionary.com

it is categorized as a verb; therefore; it is a word that implies action, just as the word *wait*.

Rest is a God-given gift for you to recover strength as you continue walking in your promise. It is not the lack of action but taking the action to relax, stay still and renew your strength. Rest was a word that was difficult for me. Physically and mentally. If you know me on a personal level, you know that my mind races a thousand miles an hour and that it is difficult for me to stay still. Having a c-section left me no choice but to learn how to rest. When I started to become forgetful of simple life details after severe migraines due to post-partum pre-eclampsia, I learned to mentally rest. When I would think of the multiple reasons why God was "punishing" me by not allowing me to get pregnant; I had to learn to rest in Him.

It was during one of my own counseling sessions after I had Isaak when I truly understood what rest meant. I was telling my counselor that I was a "runner" in life. I started school much younger than my peers and by the time I was 25, I owned my counseling practice. I feared that if I kept running at the pace that I was going, I was going to trip and fall. She asked me a simple question "do you know how runners train?". My answer was no. Although I enjoy running 5ks, I am not a trained runner. She shared with me that she was a runner and that in order for runners to train, they must slow down on occasions during the race in order to recover strength. If they continued running at the same speed, they would risk their muscles becoming hurt, thus leaving them no choice but to leave the race. This simple yet powerful analogy opened my eyes. We reached the conclusion that I was trying to run at the same speed of a previous season of my life, and it was deteriorating my spiritual, emotional and physical life. I had to slow down in order to truly reach the destination God was leading me to.

Many times all you need to do is slow down, rest, in order to recover strength so you may continue walking into God's promise for your life.

> *But those who wait on the Lord Shall renew their strength; They shall mount up with wings like eagles, They shall run and not be weary, They shall walk and not faint.* Isaiah 40:31

Rest as you wait is God's gift for you. It is the resting place where your strength will be renewed. It is in the resting place where you will be able to reach levels of intimacy with God that you have never experienced. It is after you rest when you will be able to walk confidently in what God has promised you. There is one thing that I rest in and it is that all things work for the good of those who love God and walk according to His purpose. As long as I am walking in God's purpose, I can *rest* in God's outcome, not my outcome.

## DISCERN

As you wait, you must have discernment to operate in God's kairos (timing). The word "kairos[5]" is used in the original Bible manuscript about 86 times. I became intrigued with this word as I was used to hearing it growing up in church. Kairos means an appointed time, without regard of linear time or duration of time. People refer to Kairos as being the time in which God operates as God is infinite, He is not subject to linear time. What does this mean for us and walking in our promises? We must learn that God does not operate in our Chronological Time (Chronos) and His timing is the perfect appointed time. What seems to be delayed in our time, is actually right on time for God.

Discernment will also be necessary to know which voices to listen to and which voices to ignore. Abraham, though he had a close relationship with God, failed to discern when Sarah was giving him a carnal solution.

David knew he was going to be king when the prophet Samuel came to his father's house to anoint him. However, it took him about 15 years years before he became king over all Israel. As Isaiah 40:31 *"those who wait upon the Lord, shall renew their strength"*. God will give you the strength to wait. Sometimes is the strength to endure a given situation. At times it will be the strength to not make a foolish decisions

---

[5]https://www.gotquestions.org/kairos-meaning.html

due to desperation. Just because you are waiting doesn't mean that you are not preparing for the arrival of the promise. I remember starting to prepare my body for pregnancy by taking prenatal vitamins and eating healthier. By the time I got pregnant, I had lost 10 pounds and had developed daily behaviors that allowed me to be well physically and mentally in order to carry my child to term. Lack of preparation could sometimes lead to premature labor of your promise. David's 15 years of waiting could be considered to be his "gestational" time before he was fully ready to become king. David had to utilize discernment to not make decisions that would abort his process. David had the opportunity to kill Saul yet he knew that in doing so, he would not be faithful to his covenant with God. Sinful decisions will not get you closer to your promises.

## SERVE

Learn to serve as you wait. If you are entrusted a ministry by God, learn to serve as you wait. Serve without even expecting an earthly reward. Joshua served next to Moses and I bet he didn't know that he was going to be appointed as the next leader over the people of Israel. Serve backstage before you are even onstage. In order to be able to serve in the front lines, we must first be experts at serving backstage. Sometimes we are so quick to want promotion, we are desperate for the promise, when what God is demanding is for us to learn how to serve when no human eye is watching, when the spotlight is not on us. The heart of a true servant is a heart that serves without wanting human reward for it knows that the true reward comes from heaven. God is your portion and your reward as you wait in Him.

A true servant knows that he might have the skills and knowledge to lead but also carries the patience to wait in the time of the Lord. Serve in those areas in which you will not be quickly recognized, quickly exposed, just like David did. Before David killed Goliath, his job was to bring lunch to his brothers. Great leaders know how to serve first. It is in serving where God will bring readiness upon your life and develop the skills you need to handle the weight of your promise. It is no coincidence that David, Abraham, Moses, the Israelites and Jesus had to wait prior to walking into their promise.

## PRAISE

Praise as you wait; praise God as if you already have your promise. Pastor Tony used to always say that us Christians are opposite of the world. Believers praise God before they even have the promise, the world praises or rejoices after they have received what has been promised. I invite you to praise God as if you can already see the promised land, as if you are already holding your baby, as if you are already a business owner, as if you are already fully operating in your calling, as if you already have your dream house. Learn to dance in the desert. The desert in between the promise doesn't have to be the end of you. It represents the freedom that you have obtained. It represents that you are no longer a slave of the Egyptians that kept you captive and you are on your way to greater territories, to the beautiful land of milk and honey that God has prepared for you.

## DANCE

Dance in the desert. As stated before, the process is necessary. Something that God taught me is that you cannot truly appreciate the rain of His blessings unless you have been through a drought. Your "dry" moments will teach you to appreciate the blessings that are to come. It will give you a different outlook of the awaited promise. The driest seasons of your life can increase your thirst for the Living Water; Jesus. When you can't find satisfaction on things of this world, God's living water will be your satisfaction in the midst of your desert. He never runs dry! Dance in the rain of the blessings He provides in the midst of your drought. Praise like never before because although you are not in the promised land, you are free from captivity! We take that for granted. I may not be where God promised me to be just yet but I am free from the bondage of sin. That in itself is the greatest gift of all. Jesus has turned your mourning into dancing!

## PRAY

Remember to pray as you wait. Do not get tired of praying for that awaited promise. There was a time in which I stopped praying to get pregnant. I fell under the thinking error that God already knew what I wanted; therefore, I needed to stop asking. Disbelief started to creep in and I stopped asking God for my baby. It was one day when I realized that God wanted to hear my prayers, no matter how many times I prayed for the same thing. The amount of our prayers is not meant to twist God's arm but He does delight in hearing the Righteous (1 Peter 3:12). We must also remember that the sole purpose of prayer is not to ask but also to give thanks and to hear from the Father. Let your prayer life change. Start giving thanks for your promise and seek to become intimate with Jesus in your prayer life. There are many secrets Holy Spirit wants to share with us that He will share as we seek Him in prayer.

## MEDITATE ON THE WORD

Last but not least, meditate on the Word of God as you wait. Psalm 1:1-3 states that those who delight in the law of the Lord are like a tree planted along the riverbank. As you meditate on the words that God has spoken over your life, you will be stable, you will be grounded, you will be nourished just as tree is steadily planted by the riverbank. You will not be greatly shaken. The winds may blow, the storm may rise up but you are planted in the infallible word of God. To meditate means to deeply focus on a thought. It is easy to meditate on thoughts that do not align with the word of God.  Stop meditating on what you don't have and start meditating in God's promises. I have shared before that something that helped me was to write down God's promises for my life. Create a "vision board" full of promises. Even when you don't see it in the physical sense, you can always look at that vision board for it to serve as a reminder of the Word of God. Immerse yourself in the word of God, day in and day out. When a negative thought comes, reframe your mind and focus on what God truly says.

To conclude, waiting does not equal paralysis. Ask for wisdom and direction from God. James 1:5 says that if anyone lacks wisdom, they can ask God and God will be give it liberally.  Wisdom is at your disposition when you ask with the right motives and when you ask with a humble heart. Ask God to show you areas that you still need to prepare yourself in order to be ready to receive your promises. It could be preparing your heart, preparing your mind or even preparing yourself physically.

Ask God to show you the comfort of resting in Him. Have an open ear to the Holy Spirit so you may discern which thoughts come from God and which ones are not founded on his word. Praise God as if you are holding the promise. After all, it is already within you. Dance in the midst of your driest desert. Pray fervently for He hears your cry. Always meditate on His Word alone.

I AM DESTINED FOR ISAAC

# Chapter 6

# PROMISE FULFILLED

*The Lord kept his word and did for Sarah exactly what he had promised. 2 She became pregnant, and she gave birth to a son for Abraham in his old age. This happened at just the time God had said it would. 3 And Abraham named their son Isaac. 4 Eight days after Isaac was born, Abraham circumcised him as God had commanded. 5 Abraham was 100 years old when Isaac was born.* Genesis 21:1-5

At the "end" of the story of Abraham and Sarah, God did exactly what he had promised, just as the Word said. God brought Sarah through the process of becoming pregnant and birth. I can only imagine how much more difficult it would have been for Sarah to be pregnant let alone give birth without an epidural in her old age. I love how the word says "this happened at just the time God said it would". What a reassurance. God is never too early or too late. He is just on time.

Abraham fulfilled his part of the covenant. He named his son Isaac and he followed through the circumcision, as it was commanded of him by God. It is important to know that once your promise arrives, your gratitude will be demonstrated by continuing to live a life of obedience. It was Abraham's faith and obedience that accounted him as righteous, not him receiving the promise.

## NOT THE END

Isaac is here, now what? The promise does not end with the birth of Isaac. I purposely placed quotation marks around the word "end" on the previous paragraph because Isaac's birth was not the ending, it was just the beginning. There is much more! The birth of Isaac was just the beginning of God's master plan for the life of Abraham, Sarah and the generations to come. When God grants you the blessing of fulfilling His promise, you must cherish it, take care of it, and use it to bless others rather than to keep it all for yourself.

When God allows you to become a parent, you must instruct that child in the path of the Lord, always reminding him of his or her identity, always remembering that he's a gift from the Almighty. Do not take your promise for granted for it was by God's grace it was given, not for your own merit. If it was by merit, I do not deserve to be the mother of such a beautiful little boy. I was not the motherly type to begin with. I am not perfect and in my imperfection

I have learned to cherish my child even more as I know that he was a gift out of pure grace.

When God grants your promise, it will be a blessing to those around you. I cannot begin to tell you what a blessing my Isaak has been to those around him. He did not only come to brighten my life but also the life of everyone who meets him. There are many other blessings God has granted me that have come to bless those around me; even those who did not believe the promise would come to pass.

## HOPE

There is hope even if you made some mistakes on the path to your promise. I once heard the title of "Daughters of Eve" being discussed to be the name of a conference. My pastor at the time was saying that people hear that name and they cringe at the sound of it. I cringed myself but almost immediately the Lord reminded me that Eve's mistake should not be what defines her. Her mistake did not interfere with the fulfillment of a promise rather it gave birth to a redemption plan through Jesus Christ. This is not to say that God made Eve sin in order to bring forth His plan for redemption. However, God is the mender of all things that are broken and there is no mess so big that God cannot fix in our lives. Do not let the guilt of your mistake lead you astray from the path as you walk into your promise. Do not let the guilt of your mistake allow you to not enjoy the path to your promise. Once you come to repentance, God forgives you and there is no condemnation.

## SHE (HE) LAUGHS

*And Sarah declared, "God has brought me laughter.[a] All who hear about this will laugh with me.* Genesis 21:6

The Isaacs (promises) birthed out of God's own heart will be the ones to bring joy and laughter, which is the meaning of the name Isaac. Joy does not mean that there will not be hiccups along the way. Joy means that despite of what you see, despite of life's hardship, you are able to remain content and trustful in the plan that God has for your life. Joy is waking up in the morning with hope for the future. Joy is this constant feeling of elation that is not moved by circumstances because you know who is your foundation, Jesus Christ. Joy is feeling at peace when all around you is chaos because *"Those who trust in the Lord are like Mount Zion, Which cannot be moved, but abides forever"* (Psalms 125:1).

Sarah's life was full of laughter the minute that her promise was fulfilled. She recognized that her Isaac was not only bringing her joy but was going to bring joy to those around her. Joy is contagious! Another verse that captivates my attention regarding laughter is Proverbs 31:25.

*She is clothed with strength and dignity,  and she laughs without fear of the future.* Proverbs 31:25

When you are about to give birth to your promise, the least you want to do is laugh. It is painful. The process can be lengthy, desperating, and full of uncertainty. Yet, when you are grounded in your foundation, Jesus, you are able to laugh without fear of the future. When your promise arrives, you may be scared that something may happen to it. Yet, there is no room for fear in joy.

Just looking intently into the phrase "she laughs" I realized, I have laughed many times yet not always without fear of the future. I have laughed in disbelief and doubt once, just like I shared earlier in this book. I laughed just like Sarah did the first time.

I said it before, I laughed when a prophet told my best friend that young couples in my church would conceive soon. I had been trying and nothing, so of course I laughed in disbelief at that moment. A month later I was pregnant. I can laugh about it now. I can laugh confidently that God fulfills His promise. And guess what? My son's name is Isaak, which means *laughter*. I am even laughing as I type because there was no coincidence in God's plan. He knew I needed a daily reminder to laugh.

I laughed when I did a pregnancy test and the control line wouldn't show, indicating that the test was invalid; it was neither positive or negative. I laughed and told God "you are going to make me wait, aren't you?". This time I laughed because I was close to my promise. I laughed when the same pregnancy test showed a positive result two days later!

God turned my "she laughs" of disbelief into a "she laughs" without fear of the future. I used to be a "control freak", always having a timeline for every detail of my life. Yet, God laughed at my plans and carried out His own in my life. That was when my laugh of disbelief turned into fearless laughter. I understood that I no longer needed to be a "control freak" because my future was completely secured in God. I laugh every time God confirms a word through someone because it is never something he hasn't shown me before through prayer. His word will come to pass, the future is not scary anymore.

I invite you to laugh today. Let those around you question why you are laughing in the midst of the toughest circumstances. There is no devil nor storm that can take away the laughter of those who have their future secured in Christ. Laugh without fear of the future. Maybe you laughed in disbelief once, yet God can transform that laughter into a fearless laughter as you ground yourself in His presence. When uncertainty comes, laugh. When anxiety strikes, laugh. When trials rise up, laugh. When loneliness hits, laugh. When sadness overtakes you, laugh. When anger overwhelms you, laugh. Laugh without fear of the future, God's got your back!

## "I DON'T GIVE DEAD PROMISES"

As I was pregnant with my son, a random thought of me giving birth to him dead would often come to mind. It would instantly lead to fear. One Sunday morning as I was close to my due date, I was in the middle of a beautiful "God moment" and the enemy attacked me with this thought. Instead of constantly meditating on such thought, I listened to God's voice as he told me, "I do not give dead promises". This blew my mind! God was reminding me, once again, that the promise I was carrying in my womb was not dead and I was not going to give birth to a dead promise. This situation also made me realize that perhaps the fear also stemmed from having to place my full trust in what I cannot see. I couldn't *see* that my son was doing well. Sure, I could feel him kick here and there but I just couldn't see him and that part would sometimes drive me crazy. I had to keep reminding myself that if God gave him to me, God was going to make sure he was well and even if he wasn't, to God be the glory because I carried the promise of the Lord within me. This took my faith to a new level. I was reminded that I needed to place my faith in what I cannot see, in who I cannot physically see, which is God Himself.

This statement had come to mind once again when things got complicated during my labor. There was a point that Isaak's heartbeat dropped along with my blood pressure. It was in that moment that I had to remember what God had whispered once, "I do not give dead promises". In the moment of powerlessness, I had to put my full trust in God.

Your fulfilled promise is not the end, it is just the beginning. Even when the promise is fulfilled you may experience moments of difficulty. My promise fulfilled has built some qualities in me that I wasn't even aware God had placed in me. I am more patient, I am more compassionate. My level of empathy has grown in such a way that I tear up easily (this has never happened before). It is all because I have learned to see the beauty of God's grace through the fulfillment of my promise and how it has transformed my life and the lives of those around me. Keep setting your eyes on Jesus after your promise is fulfilled. He will give you the strength to carry on.

# Chapter 7

# I AM DESTINED FOR ISAAC

*7 Who would have said to Abraham that Sarah would nurse a baby? Yet I have given Abraham a son in his old age!"*
Genesis 21:7

Abraham was destined for Isaac since the time of his birth. His name means exalted father. From the beginning of his life, God had already determined a plan to fulfill His promise in his life. God has already deposited the identity that you need to carry His promises. Maybe your literal name does not point to your identity but that is what I love about Jesus. He is in the business of changing names! It happens multiple times in the Bible. Do not see yourself through the eyes of what you are not but through the eyes of Jesus. 2 Corinthians 5:17 says "This means that anyone who belongs to Christ has become a new person. The old life is gone; a new life has begun!"

Many will watch in awe of what the Lord has done in your

life. They will say "who would have said?" My reply to that statement is "God said". If God said it, there is no one that can come against His word.

## IT TAKES A VILLAGE

As I meditated on the previous statement, the words of my best friend, Veronica, come to mind. On one occasion, she told me that she missed being pregnant with me but then she said "It is crazy because we were in the journey of being pregnant together and it was awesome but as I was thinking about it, I had to leave the journey before you". Just right after the conversation was as if the Spirit just told me, "you will be in processes with people but there will be a time where you would need to depart from the process before that person." I replied saying to Veronica, "sometimes you need to leave the process so you guide others through their own process". Do not get discouraged when others receive their promise or even a miracle before you. On the contrary, them obtaining their promise before you can help equip and prepare you for when you get your promise.

We have heard many times that it takes a village to raise a child. But I would like to add that it also takes a village to raise your promise, to develop your ministry, to build your business; it takes a village to carry out God's mission. I can tell you that my best friend being a month ahead of me in the journey of motherhood has helped me in countless ways. I have an idea of what to expect of being the mother of a little boy because of her current experience. It is of such encouragement! Better yet, I get to forever be a part of her promise because I am Levi's (her son) Godmother. Many times you will be blessed and be a blessing even as you wait for your promise.

> *While walking by the Sea of Galilee, he (Jesus) saw two brothers, Simon (who is called Peter) and Andrew his brother, casting a net into the sea, for they were fishermen.* Matthew 4:18

In Matthew 4:18, we see that Jesus recruits His first disciples and if we read before then, we notice that this happened right after Jesus came out of the desert; right after He was processed. Jesus Himself needed people to carry out God's mission for His life. You will need people, your village, to continue walking in your promise. There is power in community. When you feel exhausted or clueless as a mother or father, you will need others to remind you that if God entrusted you with that promise, He knows that through Him you will be able to handle it.

I am grateful for my village. My husband, Edgar, the one who saw the countless tears through my process yet remained believing in God's promises even when I doubted. If I am Sarah, then he is my Abraham. My Elizabeth, Veronica, my sister, who saw me pregnant when I felt the discouragement after not being pregnant myself. My parents, Javier and Lillian, who have always gone through great lengths to support me in every God-led decision. My girls, Keisha and Joanne, they are both also the best friends anyone could have. They were there when others who claimed would be there weren't. There are many other people who are part of my village, who have helped me in my walk with God. There are not enough words to express my gratitude for the "village" God has blessed me with. Two years later after I started this journey and I still have the text my best friend sent me saved, a text sent when the disappointment of not being pregnant overwhelmed me to the point of tears. It reminds me that I can't do this alone. Jesus had John the Baptist and His disciples. David needed Jonathan. Mary needed Elizabeth. Everybody needs somebody.

## HOPE AND FUTURE

Abraham took matters in his own hands and created a situation in his household that impacted the generations to come until this day. We must ask for discernment to know which things we are commanded to do and those who only God can do in our lives. We have all been Abraham at some point though, and even for that, God forgives us when we come to Him in repentance.

Even if you give birth to an Ishmael, remain faithful to God, just like Abraham did, for your promise will impact generations to come. I know that in Abraham's case, Ishmael gave birth to a generation outside of God's promise but we must not neglect to focus on what was birthed through Isaac.  From Isaac, a new generation was risen and such generation became a participant of Abraham's promise.

Your promises are not time bound, are not science bound, are not logic bound. God had to teach Abraham that his promise was going to come in his timing; at the appointed time. Remember, we operate on Kronos, God operates on Kairos. There is not a single thing that a mere human can do to rush God or twist His arm.  Your actions will not make God's promise to be fulfilled sooner than they were already determined to be fulfilled yet it is your responsibility to walk in such promise. That is the beauty of the paradox of God's Sovereignty. Don't rush the process, learn to walk through it.

Do not be fooled by the lies of the enemy telling you that God's promises will not come to pass. We must remember that He who promised is faithful (Hebrews 10:23) and the *"one who calls you is faithful and He will do it"* (1 Thessalonians 5:24). This is the Bible verse I clung to negative pregnancy test after negative pregnancy test; month after month. God said I would become a mother, I knew I would sooner or later.

*And Abraham named their son Isaac.* Genesis 21:3

Isaac was the son of the promise. Such covenant was extended to you and I through the sacrifice of Christ.  Let us patiently wait for the Isaacs in our lives because they are the ones who will bring joy and laughter. Like I said before, the meaning of the name Isaac is "laughter". That's what the fulfilled promise of God brings. There will be bumps on the road yet it will ultimately lead to a path of joy.  The Isaacs in your life are the ones who seal your covenant with God.

> *And you, dear brothers and sisters, are children of the promise, just like Isaac.  But you are now being persecuted by those who want you to keep the law, just as Ishmael, the child born by human effort, persecuted Isaac, the child born by the power of the Spirit.* Galatians 4:28-29

Everything that is birthed from God's heart is greater than anything that is birthed from our flesh. By the power of the Spirit and the work of Christ, you have been made a child of the promise, just like Isaac. The desires of your flesh may persecute you to distract you from the promise, yet remember that the promises birthed through God will prevail.

If you are reading this and you have not accepted Christ as your Savior, I invite you to partake on the greatest promise of all; Eternal Life. Romans 10:9 says "if you confess with your mouth that Jesus is Lord and believe in your heart that God raised Him from the dead, you will be saved". All you have to do is come to an understanding that you are in need of a savior, confess that Jesus is your Savior, believe and pursue a life of holiness.

I invite you to connect with a community of individuals who will walk with you to your promise. None of us can do this alone; I sure couldn't. Connect with a community that reminds you what you were destined for when the enemy tries to distract you from knowing your true identity and purpose. Submerge yourself in the Word of God as it is a daily reminder of His promises. Walk closely with the Holy Spirit and pursue holiness. Walk in your promise. Do not ever forget, you are destined for Isaac.

# EPILOGUE

By the time I finished this book, Isaak, my son, is one year old. Two years have passed since I started to write this book and all I can confidently say is that God is faithful. He reminded me of His promise, He got me through the birth of my promise and continues guiding me as I walk in the journey of parenting and the many other promises he has established for my life. Walking in God's promises has not been an easy journey yet worth it. I now know of God's faithfulness like never before. The year 2017 changed my life and showed me to wait, walk, rest and praise through my process. I continue to pray that this book is a blessing to each reader and that it draws you closer to the God who is Faithful. Your story has not ended, it's just beginning.